Workbook

Fashion Marketing & Merchandising

Mary G. Wolfe
St. Michaels, Maryland

Publisher
The Goodheart-Willcox Company, Inc.
Tinley Park, Illinois
www.g-w.com

Introduction

This workbook is designed for use with the text, *Fashion Marketing & Merchandising*. The activities included in this workbook are divided into chapters that correspond to each of the chapters in the text. Completing the activities will help you to better understand and remember the many fashion merchandising concepts and facts presented in the text.

This workbook contains a variety of activities. Some of them, such as matching exercises, have "right" answers. These activities can be used to help you review for tests and quizzes. Other activities ask for opinions, evaluations, and conclusions that cannot be judged as "right" or "wrong." These activities are designed to encourage you to consider alternatives, evaluate situations thoughtfully, and apply information in the text—often related to your own life or future.

The activities in this workbook have been designed to be both interesting and fun to do, as well as educational. This workbook will help you apply business principles and knowledge to your lifetime work, whether you choose to pursue a career in the fashion industry or in business- or marketing-related endeavors in other industries.

Table of Contents

Part 1 Basic Fashion and Business Concepts

Part 4   Retail Business Fundamentals

Part 5   Strategies for Retail Success

Part 6   Fashion Promotion

Part 7   Fashion Business in Today's World

8

Part 8   Your Future in the Fashion Industry

The Meaning of Clothing and Fashion

Needs for Clothing

Activity A

Chapter 1

Name _____

Date _____ **Period** _____

Clothing satisfies specific human needs. In the blanks on the left, identify the needs described in the chapter. Then describe each need, in your own words, on the lines provided. Finally, on the right, list articles of clothing that satisfy each need.

1. _____ need:

   (protection) _____

   _____

   _____

   _____

   _____

   _____

       a. (from weather) _____

       _____

       b. (from environmental dangers)

       _____

       c. (from occupational hazards)

       _____

       d. (from enemies)_____

       _____

2. _____ needs:

   (adornment) _____

   _____

   _____

   _____

   _____

       a. _____

       b. _____

   (identification)_____

   _____

   _____

   _____

   _____

   _____

       a. _____

       b. _____

(Continued)

Name _____

3. _____ needs:

(modesty) _____   a. _____

_____   b. _____

_____

_____

_____

_____

(status) _____   a. _____

_____   b. _____

_____

_____

_____

_____

Fashion Facts

Activity B   **Name** _____

Chapter 1   **Date** _____ **Period**_____

Think about and write answers to the following questions on the lines provided.

1. What do we mean when we speak of culture, and how does it relate to fashion? _____

    _____

    _____

    _____

2. How do uniforms identify people's roles? _____

    _____

    _____

    _____

3. How are dress code requirements different from uniforms? _____

    _____

    _____

    _____

4. How are dress code requirements similar to uniforms? _____

    _____

    _____

    _____

5. Explain how the apparel of most people is a combination of physical, psychological, and social needs.

    _____

    _____

    _____

6. How do you think your personal values and attitudes affect your clothing choices? _____

    _____

    _____

    _____

7. Why is it smart for fashion professionals to try to identify the values and attitudes of their customers?

    _____

    _____

    _____

(Continued)

Name_____

8. How can advertising influence people's values and attitudes? _____

_____

_____

_____

9. Explain how you think you balance conformity and individuality in your clothing. _____

_____

_____

_____

10. How do you think your personality is indicated in the way you dress? _____

_____

_____

_____

11. How do you think a friend's personality is reflected in the way he or she dresses? _____

_____

_____

_____

12. Describe an apparel item that you want but do not need. Why do you want it? Why do you not
    actually need it? _____

_____

_____

_____

13. Describe your three most recent major apparel purchases in relation to your needs and wants.

_____

_____

_____

_____

_____

_____

_____

_____

_____

_____

A Fashion Mirror

Activity C   **Name** _____

Chapter 1   **Date** _____ **Period** _____

Complete each of the following regarding fashion.

1. Why is fashion "a mirror of our times"? _____

   _____

   _____

   _____

2. What do you think people 100 years from now might think about our culture after looking at today's fashion magazines? (Consider that 100 years ago, sunbonnets, parasols, top hats, floor length skirts, and plain fabrics were common.) _____

   _____

   _____

   _____

   _____

   _____

3. As examples of our times, cut out pictures of today's apparel from fashion magazines or catalogs and mount them in the following three boxes. Write a short description of what the fashions in each picture might indicate to people in the future about our current economic conditions, political issues, technology, newsworthy events, popular entertainment, etc.

   a. _____

   _____

   _____

   _____

   _____

   _____

   _____

   _____

   _____

   _____

   _____

   _____

(Continued)

Name_____

b. _____

_____

_____

_____

_____

_____

_____

_____

_____

_____

_____

_____

_____

c. _____

_____

_____

_____

_____

_____

_____

_____

_____

_____

_____

_____

_____

Express Your Thoughts

Activity D

Chapter 1

Name _____

Date _____ Period _____

Think about the following statements, and write your reaction to each on the lines provided.

1. People who intentionally adorn themselves differently from most people may be seeking change or adventure. They might want some psychological zest or relief from boredom. _____

   _____

   _____

   _____

2. Occupational clothing is specialized attire designed to protect a worker from the hazards of a particular occupation. Dangerous jobs, such as dealing with toxic materials, infectious substances, heat or cold, etc., are becoming safer because of technology that is developing better protective apparel. _____

   _____

   _____

   _____

3. The "Hemline Index" is an old theory that says trends of hemline lengths and the level of the stock market go up and down at the same time. Although many fashion and stock market experts think this is silly and should be taken lightly, it reinforces the basic idea that people's moods are reflected in the way they dress. _____

   _____

   _____

   _____

4. During major wars, there is often a military influence on fashion designs as well as the use of materials. For instance, during World War II, the government restricted the amount of fabric available for civilian clothing because of needs for military clothing and supplies. Civilian clothes were tight, with skimpy hems and seam allowances. Men's trousers no longer had cuffs. The country's economic needs were reflected in the fashions of the time. _____

   _____

   _____

   _____

5. Uniforms have become popular in some public schools. This is enabling students to have a strong identity with their school. Students behave in more studious ways because they are dressed to do school work. Also, fewer social barriers exist because everyone is dressed similarly—without expensive garments or jewelry to cause jealousy, theft, or violence. _____

   _____

   _____

   _____

Fashion Term Matching

Activity E   **Name** _____

Chapter 1   **Date** _____ **Period** _____

Match the following terms and definitions by placing the correct letter next to each number.

_____ 1. The prevailing type of clothing that is favored by a large segment of the public at a given time.

_____ 2. The passing love for a new fashion that is accompanied by a display of emotion or crowd excitement.

_____ 3. The prevailing opinion of what is and is not attractive and appropriate for a given person and occasion.

_____ 4. An article of wearing apparel, such as a dress, suit, coat, evening gown, or sweater.

_____ 5. The articles added to complete or enhance apparel outfits.

_____ 6. Styles that are produced in volume and widely sold at lower prices.

_____ 7. A particular, or unique, version of a style.

_____ 8. Components of garments, such as the sleeves, cuffs, collar, waistband, etc.

_____ 9. A design, shape, or type of apparel item distinguished by the particular characteristics that make it unique.

_____ 10. Items of the very latest or newest fashions.

_____ 11. A temporary, passing fashion that has great appeal to many people for a short period of time.

_____ 12. A style or design that continues to be popular over an extended period of time, even though fashions change.

_____ 13. A total accessorized outfit.

_____ 14. The most daring and wild designs.

A. accessories
B. avant-garde
C. classic
D. craze
E. design
F. fad
G. fashion
H. fashion look
I. garment
J. garment parts
K. high fashion
L. mass fashion
M. style
N. taste

Fashion Movement

Fashion Myths and Truths

Activity A

Chapter 2

Name _____

Date _____ Period _____

After reading each of the following statements, indicate if you think the statement is a *myth* or a *truth* by checking the appropriate column. Then turn to the back of this page to check your answers. In the space provided, select a statement that is a *truth* and expand upon it, giving examples of why it is a *truth*. Later, discuss all of the statements as a class.

	Myth	Truth
1. The pace of fashion change is related to the overall pace of the culture.	_____	_____
2. Fashion trends are less noticeable today because consumers are more likely to stick to their own preferences rather than always buying the latest fashions.	_____	_____
3. Fashion designers and retailers dictate what is fashionable by forcing new fashions on consumers. The resulting obsolescence causes people to feel they must buy new items.	_____	_____
4. Every fashion is eventually adopted by all groups of the population.	_____	_____
5. More fashions and types of clothes are popular at the same time now, than in the past, because of people's varied lifestyles.	_____	_____
6. Fashion movement mainly influences women.	_____	_____
7. Fashion trends are recurring faster in this century than they did in past centuries.	_____	_____
8. Fashion is a mysterious and unpredictable force.	_____	_____
9. The fashion industry is harmful because it encourages people to buy things they do not need and to replace items before they are worn out.	_____	_____
10. The three groups that simultaneously cause fashion change are fashion businesses, fashion innovators, and consumers.	_____	_____

Statement number _____ is a truth for the following reasons:

_____

_____

_____

_____

(Continued)

Name_____

1. *Truth.* If the culture remains the same, fashion change is slow because people continue to wear traditional apparel rather than desiring new fashion trends.

2. *Truth.* It is now common to see skirts of all lengths being worn and older apparel items that are comfortable. Less social pressure dictates fashions these days.

3. *Myth.* Consumers actually need variety. They "vote" with their purchases of the designs that become fashions, thus accepting or rejecting the styles that are offered.

4. *Myth.* Acceptance is not universal among all segments of the population. For instance, high school and college fashions are usually very different from business attire. City and suburban fashions differ because of different lifestyles. Also, a style may be accepted and become a fashion in one part of the world while it is ignored or rejected elsewhere.

5. *Truth.* People need wardrobes for their various careers, athletic activities, social events, and all the other different uses for their time.

6. *Myth.* Men and children are influenced, too. They buy ties of new widths or patterns, decide about jeans or pleated pants, want certain colors/fabrics/fit in their garments, etc. Children want to look like their peers. The menswear industry has grown faster than womenswear recently.

7. *Truth.* In past centuries, fashion looks recurred about every 100 years, but now they are seen again about every generation.

8. *Myth.* The direction of fashion can be predicted with some accuracy by those who study and understand its fundamentals. Besides having artistic content, fashion movement can be scientifically measured and evaluated.

9. *Myth.* The activities of the fashion industry stimulate our economy, helping manufacturers and retailers to be successful, and creating jobs.

10. *Truth.* Fashion movement is a combination of the actions of all three groups that together create, promote, sell, and buy new fashions.

Working with Fashion Movement

Activity B   **Name** _____

Chapter 2   **Date** _____ **Period**_____

Respond to each of the following regarding fashion movement.

1. Why does fashion movement exist? _____

    _____

    _____

    _____

2. Describe how fashion leaders promote the movement of fashion. _____

    _____

    _____

    _____

3. Explain why, unlike antiques, fashion items do not improve with age. _____

    _____

    _____

    _____

4. Draw a merchandise acceptance curve on top of this sample fashion cycle for descriptions a, b, and c. Use a different color pencil for each, or put an "a," "b," or "c" on each, or key your lines in another way.

    a. a style that is accepted quickly, maintains general popularity for some time, and then drops from popularity quickly.

    b. a style that is accepted slowly, maintains general popularity for only a short time, and then drops from popularity slowly.

    c. a style that is accepted quickly to a certain extent, then its popularity wanes, but it gains great acceptance later, before finally losing popularity quite suddenly.

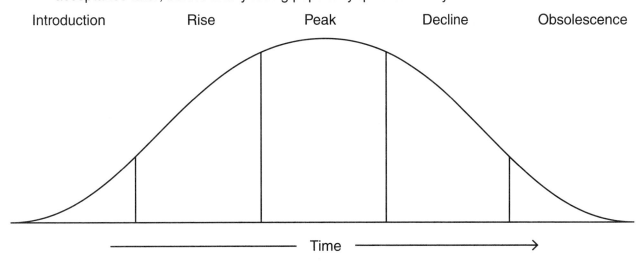

Introduction   Rise   Peak   Decline   Obsolescence

Time ——————————————————→

Relating to Fashion Leaders and Followers

Activity C   **Name** _____

Chapter 2   **Date** _____ **Period** _____

Complete each of the following items related to fashion leaders and followers.

1. Respond to this statement: "Because most consumers are fashion followers, fashion designers and apparel manufacturers tend to copy, adapt, or update recently accepted fashions." _____

   _____

   _____

   _____

2. Do you think you are a fashion leader, fashion follower, or fashion lagger? Explain and use examples.

   _____

   _____

   _____

   _____

3. Study a fashion leader of the past. (Examples might include French royalty of the 15th or 16th centuries, Marie Antoinette, Audrey Hepburn, Doris Day, Twiggy, Jacqueline Kennedy, Elvis Presley, Michael Jackson, Madonna, Joan Collins, Princess Diana, Nancy Reagan, etc.) Write a brief report here about the fashion trends that person started and the influence on the apparel industry and lifestyles of the times. _____

   _____

   _____

   _____

   _____

   _____

   _____

   _____

   _____

   _____

   _____

   _____

   _____

   _____

   _____

Analyzing Today's Fashion Trends

Activity D   **Name** _____

Chapter 2   **Date** _____ **Period**_____

Respond to each of the following regarding today's fashion trends.

1. Analyze the current (or upcoming) fashion season by looking at fashion publications, reports of designer collections, and retail advertising. Also, if possible, watch TV fashion news, visit stores, and interview merchandisers. Write your findings about the trends here. Attach pictures or sketches to illustrate your points.

   Silhouettes (shapes)

   _____

   _____

   Colors

   _____

   _____

   Garment part details

   _____

   _____

   Fabrics/textures

   _____

   _____

   Prints/patterns

   _____

   _____

   Accessories (footwear, jewelry, handbags, etc.)

   _____

   _____

   Other

   _____

   _____

2. Describe a current fashion trend that illustrates the trickle-down theory. _____

   _____

   _____

   _____

   _____

(Continued)

Name_____

3. Describe a current fashion trend that illustrates the trickle-across theory. _____

_____

_____

_____

_____

_____

_____

4. Describe a current fashion trend that illustrates the trickle-up theory. _____

_____

_____

_____

_____

_____

_____

5. Describe an example of a classic garment that is especially popular today. _____

_____

_____

_____

_____

_____

_____

6. Describe an example of a recent fad that is past its fashion cycle peak. _____

_____

_____

_____

_____

_____

_____

Some Terms to Ponder

Activity E   **Name** _____

Chapter 2   **Date** _____ **Period**_____

Think about the definitions for the following terms, checking certain terms in the dictionary if needed. Then paraphrase each definition (write it differently in your own words) and describe any current or past (or possible future!) fashion looks that fit the term.

1. Prophetic styles—New styles, still in the introductory stage of their fashion cycles, that are noted by forecasters as possible future trends and possibly even mass fashions to come.

   _____

   _____

   _____

   _____

2. Recurring fashions—Styles that go in and out of fashion acceptance regularly, but do not maintain constant acceptance like classics.

   _____

   _____

   _____

   _____

   _____

3. Androgynous dressing—Wearing clothes that are neither specifically feminine nor masculine.

   _____

   _____

   _____

   _____

   _____

4. Anti-fashion—Dressing specifically to look unfashionable.

   _____

   _____

   _____

   _____

   _____

(Continued)

Name _____

5. <u>Fashion monger</u>—One who attempts to stir up, spread, or sell petty or discreditable fashion ideas or merchandise.

_____

_____

_____

_____

6. <u>Fashion plate</u>—Someone who is always perfectly outfitted with the latest fashion attire.

_____

_____

_____

_____

7. <u>Campus fashion</u>—Accepted looks for students at certain schools, regardless of the dictates of generally accepted fashion.

_____

_____

_____

_____

8. <u>Diffusion</u>—Movement of fashions toward wide acceptance, especially by being copied at lower price levels.

_____

_____

_____

_____

Basic Economic Concepts

Understanding Free-Market Concepts

Activity A   Name _____

Chapter 3   Date _____ Period_____

Complete the following exercises about free-market concepts.

1. This most basic illustration of a **market** (where sellers and buyers make transactions) shows one person who only raises food products, another who only makes clothes, and another who only builds houses. Tell how, by using a free-market system, the three people can satisfy their needs for food, clothing, and shelter.

   "A" only raises food

   "B" only makes clothes

   MARKET

   "C" only builds houses

   _____

   _____

   _____

   _____

   _____

2. Look up the meaning of *benefits* in the dictionary. Then describe the statement, "Products are bundles of benefits." _____

   _____

   _____

   _____

   _____

3. Using an example of a specific fashion item (pair of jeans, coat, etc.), list at least three benefits it provides to the user.

   Product: _____

   Benefits: _____

   _____

   _____

   _____

(Continued)

Name _____

4. It costs a manufacturer $60 per dozen to make a specific sweater, and the manufacturer sells 3,000 dozen at $100 per dozen. (Show your calculations.)

   a. What is the profit for each dozen sold? $ _____ profit per dozen

   b. What is the total profit from the sweaters? $ _____ total profit

5. If that same manufacturer miscalculates the demand of the market and manufactures 5,000 dozen of those sweaters, but only sells 3,000 dozen, what is the total profit from the sweaters? (Show your calculations.) $ _____ profit.

6. From the example above, explain why it is important for companies to try to predict supply and demand as accurately as possible. _____

   _____

   _____

7. Relating to supply and demand, how might a sweater manufacturing company consider adjusting its selling price the next season (raising or lowering) if:

   a. There are fewer sweaters being produced by other companies? _____

   Why? _____

   b. There are more sweaters being produced by other companies? _____

   Why? _____

   c. Fleece jackets are gaining popularity instead of sweaters? _____

   Why? _____

8. It costs XYZ Retail Store $20 to stock and sell each pair of jeans, and the store sells 75 pairs of jeans per month at $30 per pair.

   a. What is the profit for each pair sold? $ _____ profit per pair

   b. What is the monthly profit from selling the jeans? $ _____ monthly profit

(Continued)

Name _____

9. It costs Jones Retail Store $28 to stock and sell each pair of winter boots, and the store usually sells 180 pairs of boots at $40 each during the January/February time period.

   a. What is the store's usual total profit for selling those boots during that period? $ _____

   b. If the winter is mild and dry, thus lowering the demand for boots, the store might have to reduce the price of those boots to sell them. If the store sells 100 pairs at $32 each during January, and the remaining 80 pairs at a final clearance sale price of $25 each in February, what is the total profit for selling the boots? $ _____ total profit

10. Because of the disappointing sales of boots in the previously described mild, dry winter, plus a price increase to stock and sell each pair of winter boots, all retail stores in town order fewer pairs of boots the next year. Jones Retail Store orders 150 pairs at a cost of $30 each. However, last minute predictions for a bad winter, plus pent-up needs from consumers who did not get boots the year before, have been miscalculated by the retailers.

   a. What has happened to the supply and the demand for boots? _____
   _____

   b. If Jones Retail Store is able to sell all 150 pairs of boots at the higher price of $55 each, what is the store's total profit for the boots? $ _____ profit

   c. Jones Retail Store would have been able to sell 50 more pairs of boots at that price, if they were available in store inventory, which means they missed the opportunity to make how much more profit? $ _____ unrealized profit (called opportunity cost)

11. Why is competition good for the economy? _____
   _____
   _____
   _____
   _____

12. How does competition raise the standard of living of consumers? _____
   _____
   _____
   _____

Economic Terms Crossword

Activity B

Chapter 3

Name _____

Date _____   Period_____

Complete this crossword puzzle using the clues listed.

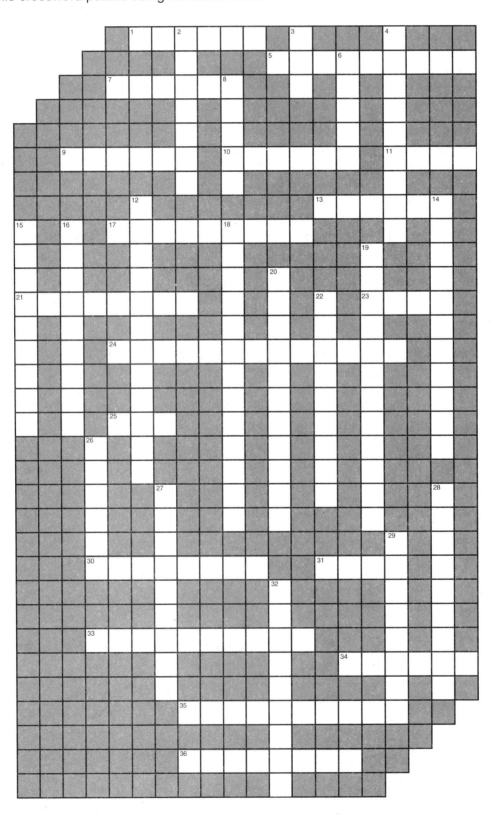

(Continued)

Name _____

Across

1. Quantities of a good or service that producers are willing and able to provide at a particular time at various prices.
5. Shareholders of corporations have the advantage of limited _____, or the legal responsibility for debts and obligations.
7. The level of necessities and luxuries enjoyed by a population for various levels of comfort and status is their standard of _____.
9. The block of consumers that a company wants as customers, and toward whom it directs its marketing efforts, is called a _____ market.
10. The amounts of a good or service that consumers are willing and able to buy at a certain time and price.
11. In the market structure of _____ competition, no company in an industry is large or powerful enough to influence or control prices.
13. Companies that offer their stock to the general public, usually on national exchanges, are known as _____ corporations.
17. People who buy and use finished products.
21. A market structure in which there is only one company that controls an industry.
23. A _____ proprietorship business is owned by just one person.
24. Companies that make goods.
25. A _____-profit corporation exists to provide a social service rather than to make a profit.
30. The marketing _____ relates price to volume, showing that lower priced products will sell in larger quantities than higher priced products.
31. In the _____-market system, the way people spend their money determines which products will be produced and what the products will cost.
33. Times of economic decrease in national income, employment, and production.
34. Business _____ are ongoing fluctuations in the level of economic activity over periods of several years.
35. Periods of economic growth in national income, employment, and production.
36. Economic goods or services that fulfill a market need and are exchanged for payment.

Down

2. The stock of _____ corporations is not available to the general public.
3. A marketing _____ is a blend of product, price, place, and promotion that satisfies a chosen market.
4. A market structure with only a few large rival firms that produce the products, dominate the market, and react to each other's actions.
6. The right products being at the right place at the right time in the right quantity at the right price with the right appeal is known as the merchandise _____.
8. Physical products that are made by manufacturers.
12. Chartered enterprises organized as separate legal entities with most of the legal rights of people.
14. Rivalry between two or more independent businesses to gain as much of the total market sales, or customer acceptance, as possible.
15. Nonpersonal selling to a large audience to increase buying response.
16. _____ of scale are cost reductions per item resulting from volume mass production.
18. The process through which products are obtained and promoted to the point of sale.
19. Activities involved in physically transferring goods from where they are produced to the proper locations for consumption.
20. An unincorporated business that is co-owned and operated by two or more persons.
22. The process of finding or creating a profitable market for specific goods or services.
26. Money left over after expenses and taxes have been deducted from what was received from the company's sales.
27. Companies that sell merchandise in small quantities to end-use consumers.
28. Industrial materials and manufacturing capabilities.
29. Intangible activities or benefits that are performed and have value.
32. A sliding scale from one extreme to another with infinite possible responses falling at different points along it.

Questionable Thoughts

Activity C   **Name** _____

Chapter 3   **Date** _____   **Period** _____

Write thought-provoking multiple choice questions with information contained in any parts of the following main chapter sections. Record the correct answers on another piece of paper. Then exchange activity guide pages with a classmate, and ask your classmate to circle the letter of the correct answer for each question.

<u>The Free-Market System</u> (profit motivation, competition, supply/demand, impacts on society):

1. _____

    _____

    a. _____

    b. _____

    c. _____

    d. _____

2. _____

    _____

    a. _____

    b. _____

    c. _____

    d. _____

3. _____

    _____

    a. _____

    b. _____

    c. _____

    d. _____

<u>Competitive Market Structures</u>:

4. _____

    _____

    a. _____

    b. _____

    c. _____

    d. _____

(Continued)

Name _____

Basic Forms of Business Organizations (sole proprietorships, partnerships, corporations):

5. _____

   _____

   a. _____

   b. _____

   c. _____

   d. _____

6. _____

   _____

   a. _____

   b. _____

   c. _____

   d. _____

Business Cycles:

7. _____

   _____

   a. _____

   b. _____

   c. _____

   d. _____

The Concept of Marketing (product, price, place, promotion):

8. _____

   _____

   a. _____

   b. _____

   c. _____

   d. _____

(Continued)

Name _____

9. _____

_____

   a. _____

   b. _____

   c. _____

   d. _____

<u>The Concept of Merchandising</u>:

10. _____

_____

   a. _____

   b. _____

   c. _____

   d. _____

Gaining Some Business Economic Background

Activity D   **Name** _____

Chapter 3   **Date** _____ **Period**_____

Complete the following exercises about business economics.

1. Define *liability*. _____

2. Active business owners are called <u>principals</u> of their firms. Look up *principal* in the dictionary and write the version here that relates to business ownership. _____

   _____

   _____

3. Describe what the liability is for a principal or shareholder in each of the following forms of business:

   a. Sole proprietorship _____

   _____

   b. Partnership _____

   _____

   c. Corporation _____

   _____

4. What are business cycles? _____

   _____

   _____

5. In relation to business cycles, what is a *recession*? _____

   _____

   _____

6. What types of apparel items do consumers mainly buy during recessions? _____

   _____

   _____

7. In relation to business cycles, what is an *expansion*? _____

   _____

   _____

8. What types of apparel items do consumers mainly buy during expansions? _____

   _____

   _____

(Continued)

Name_____

9. In the library or on the Internet, look up information about the government's Index of Leading Economic Indicators. Explain how often it is reported, what it predicts, and any other facts of interest. _____

_____

_____

10. Look up information about the gross domestic product (GDP). Describe what the GDP measures, and its significance. _____

_____

_____

_____

11. What is a company's target market? _____

_____

_____

_____

12. Cut out and mount two fashion advertisements here. Briefly describe the group of consumers you believe to be the target market for each ad. Explain your reasoning.

    a. _____

        _____

        _____

        _____

        _____

        _____

        _____

        _____

    b. _____

        _____

        _____

        _____

        _____

        _____

        _____

        _____

Economic Questions

Activity E   **Name** _____

Chapter 3   **Date** _____ **Period** _____

Complete the following exercises about economics.

1. To illustrate how **economies of scale are efficient because fixed costs** (expenses that must be paid regardless of how much is sold) **are spread among more goods being produced**, compute the following:

   It costs a manufacturer $500,000 per year <u>fixed costs</u> to pay rent, utilities, management salaries, and other overhead, regardless of how many dresses are made and sold.

   <u>Unit costs</u> of materials (fabric, buttons, etc.) and direct labor (machine operators) are $50 to produce each dozen of all the different types of dresses in the line.

   a. If 50,000 dozen dresses are produced, the company's fixed costs spread across all of them is $10 per dozen. This results in total production costs per dozen dresses of $_____.

   b. If only 25,000 dozen dresses are produced by that same company, fixed costs spread across all of them are how much per dozen? $_____. In that case, what would the total cost be to produce each dozen dresses? $_____.

2. Explain in your own words the statement in bold print in #1 above. _____

   _____

   _____

   _____

3. Complete the following:

   a. Jones Retail Store has fixed costs of $30,000 per month to pay its mortgage, utilities, management salaries, and other overhead. The store takes in about $150,000 each month, selling about 5,000 items that have an average cost per item sold of $22. What is the store's usual profit per month?

   $_____ taken in (income)

   −$_____ fixed costs

   −$_____ total unit costs

   =$_____ profit

   b. Calculated in the average cost per item sold are unit costs for sales help, advertising, and the purchase of the goods from manufacturers. Since there is great demand for the store's goods, Jones' management has decided to double the amount of merchandise the store sells (also doubling the sales help, advertising, etc., which maintains the same unit costs). The store is successful at selling all of the goods, taking in $300,000 per month. What is the new amount of profit per month? $_____ profit

   c. Relating to economies of scale, why is the amount of profit so much more than double the previous profit?

   _____

(Continued)

Name _____

4. Why is mass production, which takes advantage of economics of scale, different from the marketing-oriented approach that is being stressed today? _____

_____

_____

_____

_____

5. Briefly justify today's marketing-oriented approach of determining customer desires before products are manufactured (as opposed to a product-oriented approach). _____

_____

_____

_____

_____

6. Define fashion marketing. _____

_____

_____

_____

_____

7. Describe the right merchandise blend. _____

_____

_____

_____

_____

8. Discuss pricing in relation to sales volume, as illustrated by the marketing triangle. _____

_____

_____

_____

_____

_____

_____

_____

_____

_____

Substance of
the Fashion
Industry

Traveling the Pipeline

Activity A   **Name** _____

Chapter 4   **Date** _____ **Period** _____

Respond to each of the following questions or statements.

1. Briefly describe the following parts of the textile/apparel pipeline:

   a. Fiber production.

   _____

   _____

   b. Yarn production.

   _____

   _____

   c. Fabric manufacturing.

   _____

   _____

   d. Fabric finishing.

   _____

   _____

   e. Apparel designing.

   _____

   _____

   f. Apparel manufacturing.

   _____

   _____

   g. Apparel sales.

   _____

   _____

(Continued)

Name_____

h. Quantity buying.

_____

_____

i. Single-item selling.

_____

_____

2. Define vertical integration. _____

_____

_____

3. Describe one advantage for apparel manufacturers that open one or more factory outlet stores.

_____

_____

_____

4. Describe one disadvantage for apparel manufacturers that open one or more factory outlet stores.

_____

_____

_____

5. What is the main advantage of private label goods for retailers? _____

_____

_____

Non-Apparel Textile Marketing

Activity B   **Name** _____

Chapter 4   **Date** _____   **Period**_____

Complete the following activities related to non-apparel textiles.

1. Cut out a picture from a magazine or catalog, or print one from the Internet, of some home furnishings textiles. Mount it in the space provided. Describe how the textiles are used for furniture, windows, domestics, floor coverings, or other decorating. Also relate your example to home "fashion trends."

_____

_____

_____

_____

_____

_____

_____

_____

_____

_____

_____

_____

_____

(Continued)

Name_____

2. Get a picture from a magazine or the Internet of a technical textile in use. Mount it in the space provided. Describe the importance of the textile for this particular use and its specialized characteristics. For what other industrial uses might a textile with these characteristics be appropriate?

_____

_____

_____

_____

_____

_____

_____

_____

_____

_____

_____

_____

_____

_____

_____

_____

Your Fashion Industry Quiz

Activity C   **Name** _____

Chapter 4   **Date** _____ **Period** _____

Write one true/false question for each of the chapter sections noted, and write the correct answers on another piece of paper. If your question is false, write the sentence as a true statement on your other piece of paper. Then exchange activity guide pages with a classmate to try to answer each other's questions correctly on this page. Check answers with the prepared answer sheet.

True or False

The Soft Goods Chain—Textile Segment:

_____ 1.

_____

_____

_____

_____

_____

The Soft Goods Chain—Apparel Segment:

_____ 2.

_____

_____

_____

_____

_____

The Soft Goods Chain—Retail Segment:

_____ 3.

_____

_____

_____

_____

_____

(Continued)

Name _____

The Four-Groups Approach:

_____ 4.

_____

_____

_____

_____

_____

Vertical Integration:

_____ 5.

_____

_____

_____

_____

_____

Commodity, Fashion, and Seasonal Goods:

_____ 6.

_____

_____

_____

_____

_____

Other Textile End-Use Industries—Household Textile Products:

_____ 7.

_____

_____

_____

_____

_____

(Continued)

Name _____

Other Textile End-Use Industries—Technical Textile Products:

_____ 8.

_____

_____

_____

_____

_____

Other Textile End-Use Industries—The Home Sewing Industry:

_____ 9.

_____

_____

_____

_____

_____

Fashion Industry Associations and/or Publications:

_____10.

_____

_____

_____

_____

_____

Geographic Locations of Industry Segments:

_____11.

_____

_____

_____

_____

_____

Read and React

Activity D   **Name** _____

Chapter 4   **Date** _____ **Period** _____

Think about the following statements and write your reaction to each on the lines provided.

1. The fashion business is unusually exciting because numerous industries in the textile/apparel
   pipeline all work together with a unique relationship to keep consumers of fashion satisfied.

   _____

   _____

2. Often several parts of the soft goods chain hold trade shows simultaneously at the same convention
   facility. An example is when international fabric suppliers, men's sportswear firms, private label
   garment manufacturers, and children's wear companies occupy different areas of the huge Javits
   Convention Center in New York City.

   _____

   _____

3. Fashion forecasters in the auxiliary group not only report on upcoming trends through newsletters
   and presentations. They also offer help by developing fabrics, designing apparel lines, and
   recommending manufacturing sources to clients who request and pay for the additional services.

   _____

   _____

4. "Factors" are financial intermediaries that facilitate the flow of money between sellers and buyers
   all through the soft goods chain. For instance, when a manufacturer sells garments to many retail
   stores, the factor pays the manufacturer a large percentage of what is owed by the retailers.
   The factor then collects the money owed from the retailers and keeps the entire amount. The
   manufacturer gets cash immediately, and the retailers pay the exact amount they owe. The factor
   earns the additional percentage as a fee for providing fast money to the seller, serving as the
   collection department, and accepting the risk of some possible nonpayment.

   _____

   _____

5. Retailers must calculate what commodity staple goods and fashion products their stores will stock.
   One more variable to the challenge of providing merchandise to the selling floor for consumer
   purchase at the optimum time is deciding when to offer specific seasonal goods.

   _____

   _____

Differences Described

Activity E   **Name** _____

Chapter 4   **Date** _____ **Period** _____

Describe the differences between the following terms.

What is the difference between:

1. Channel of distribution and the soft goods chain? _____

   _____

   _____

   _____

2. Fibers and greige goods? _____

   _____

   _____

   _____

3. Yarns and fabrics? _____

   _____

   _____

   _____

4. Wholesalers and resellers? _____

   _____

   _____

   _____

5. Primary group and secondary group of the four-groups approach? _____

   _____

   _____

   _____

6. Raw materials and fabricated products? _____

   _____

   _____

   _____

7. Retail group and auxiliary group of the four-groups approach? _____

   _____

   _____

   _____

(Continued)

Name _____

8. Forward integration and backward integration? _____

_____

_____

_____

9. Commodity products and fashion products? _____

_____

_____

_____

10. Private label goods and seasonal goods? _____

_____

_____

_____

11. Domestics and home furnishings textiles? _____

_____

_____

_____

12. Geotextiles and composites? _____

_____

_____

_____

13. Trade associations and trade publications? _____

_____

_____

_____

14. Textile performance and technical textiles? _____

_____

_____

_____

15. *Women's Wear Daily* and *STORES* trade journal? _____

_____

_____

_____

Satisfying the Fashion Market

Working with Market Share

Activity A

Chapter 5

Name _____

Date _____ Period_____

Complete the following market share exercises.

Market Size: Companies must first consider how big their market is. (Markets are not likely to be worldwide.) Indicate what geographic area probably encompasses the markets for:

1. The JCPenney Company _____

2. Susie's Dress Shoppe at 415 Main Street _____

3. The Northwest Bridal Outlet _____

Market Share: Stores share business in their market with their competition. Each company's portion of all the business is its market share.

4. With which of the above stores would Anne's Fashions of 305 Main Street compete? _____

    _____

5. With which of the above stores would Sears compete? _____

6. With which of the above stores would Greater Seattle Bride & Bridesmaid compete? _____

    _____

All of the above retailers probably also compete with many other stores within their market.

7. Some retailers have a small share of a small market. T-shirt shops at a small seasonal resort would fit this category. What might another example be? _____

    _____

8. Some retailers have a large share of a small market. These stores have tightly defined target markets and few competitors. They get most of what business exists. A cruisewear shop in a midwestern town is an example. What might another example be? _____

    _____

9. Some retailers have a small share of a large market. Small independent apparel stores often fall into this category because they compete with all other stores in a large, obvious market. Name a store in your area that you think falls within this category. _____

    _____

(Continued)

Name _____

10. Some retailers have a large share of a large market. Lands' End is a mail-order retailer that has high sales of moderately priced casualwear throughout North America and in some other parts of the world. Name a retail store company that sells high quantities of moderately priced casualwear through stores in most urban and suburban areas. _____

_____

11. How has selling over the Internet changed the scope of retail markets? _____

_____

_____

_____

Think about the following statements and write your reaction to each on the lines provided.

12. Increasing a company's market share is often considered to be a performance objective (something to strive toward), especially for small and growing retail companies. However, many companies have trouble defining their specific market, as well as their share in it. _____

_____

_____

_____

13. Market share is shown as a percentage of the entire market, calculated by dividing the firm's sales volume by the total sales volume in that category of retailing. It is usually based on dollars, but can also be calculated by number of units sold. _____

_____

_____

_____

14. The market share of all competitors can be illustrated with representative pie wedges of different sizes, as sections of a circle. If this is done each year and compared over several years, it clearly shows which firms are increasing or decreasing in market share. Sometimes trade organizations publish pie charts along with the results of market studies. _____

_____

_____

_____

15. Maximizing market share may not maximize profits beyond a certain point. If retailers must cut their selling prices and increase promotion spending to gain more market share, volume may not increase enough to result in higher overall profits. _____

_____

_____

_____

Fashion Market Research

Activity B   **Name** _____

Chapter 5   **Date** _____ **Period** _____

Properly analyzed and interpreted data about consumer purchase behavior can be a powerful tool for fashion companies. By continuously tracking consumer activity in the market, timely and accurate data is gained for better informed marketing decisions.

Many consulting firms specialize in market research. They do market analysis for specific businesses and market segments, provide data monthly or quarterly, and include charts and graphs with computer reports. They track specific brands, profile consumers of competitive products, analyze different geographic territories, and watch all demographic and psychographic movement.

Consumer panel participants fill out monthly forms on which they record all details of their purchases of apparel and home textiles. The information reported includes price, style, fabric, fiber content, size, color, brand name, country of origin, care labeling, store where purchased, and who will use each item. A large sample of participants is required for meaningful results.

Play the role of a market researcher. Cut out or print a picture of a fashion garment (appropriate for your friends) and mount it on a piece of paper. Show the picture to 20 or more different consumers in the target market (classmates, relatives, etc.), asking them questions #1-4 below and writing their answers in a notebook. Compile the results and summarize them in writing after each question on this page. Also staple or paper clip the picture of the garment to this page.

Research questions:

1. What do you like best about this fashion? _____

    _____

    _____

    _____

2. What do you like least about this fashion? _____

    _____

    _____

    _____

3. What could be done to improve this fashion? _____

    _____

    _____

    _____

4. Would you buy this fashion? Why or why not? _____

    _____

    _____

    _____

(Continued)

Name _____

Questions for you to answer:

5. Did you gain any quantitative as well as qualitative information? Explain. _____

    _____

    _____

    _____

6. If you were in charge of marketing for a clothing line, how important would it be for you to gain ongoing market research results? _____

    _____

    _____

    _____

7. How can market research help a fashion company identify new opportunities, anticipate what competitors might do, and establish realistic market share targets? _____

    _____

    _____

    _____

8. What did you learn about market research from this exercise? _____

    _____

    _____

    _____

Interest in Technology

Activity C   Name _____

Chapter 5   Date _____ Period_____

Read the following statements and indicate your reaction to each. Check if you think the statement is an interesting aspect of information technology, or if it seems uninteresting to you. You will not be graded on your responses. Then choose what you feel is the most interesting statement of the group and explain your reaction to it in detail.

Interesting   Uninteresting

_____ _____ 1. Benefits of using product codes include accuracy of data input, speed of entering data into the computer system, timeliness of information to all who need it, and labor savings from elimination of manual systems.

_____ _____ 2. "Smart-tech" thinking is that companies automate to improve consistent product quality, not just to reduce labor.

_____ _____ 3. New information technology has many advantages. However, disadvantages include the high cost of buying the systems and difficulties of installing and learning them.

_____ _____ 4. More advanced methods of product code labeling and tracking have been developed because of pressures of business partnerships.

_____ _____ 5. Companies that provide information technology also offer "user support" for instructions and help with setting up and using the product codes, printers, and other technology.

_____ _____ 6. Laser scanners have a tightly focused beam and can scan bar codes from a distance. They are quite sophisticated and expensive.

_____ _____ 7. Scanning wands are considered to be "the low-end workhorse" and are used by many fashion manufacturers and retailers.

_____ _____ 8. If computers and other technology can increase the flow of usable information to managers, better decisions can be made and company profits can improve.

_____ _____ 9. It is hard for small companies to stay up with the latest technology because they don't have the sizable financial and human resources from which to draw that large companies have.

_____ _____ 10. Prices of high-tech devices and systems are dropping rather than becoming more expensive. This enables more companies to be able to use them.

_____ _____ 11. Smaller information technology equipment is being developed all the time that is faster, more accurate, and lighter in weight.

_____ _____ 12. The Association for Retail Technology Standards (ARTS) has developed open computer system standards so components of most systems can interact with each other.

_____ _____ 13. Wireless (through the air) scanning allows for information to be sent from remote locations to the "host" computer.

(Continued)

Name_____

_____   _____   14. Most consumers are familiar with the usual "linear" bar codes. New radio frequency identification (RFID) codes that hold larger amounts of data are sometimes round or square.

_____   _____   15. After spending millions of dollars on hardware and software over the past few decades, some companies ask why their productivity and profits have not drastically improved. However, they have been able to successfully compete.

_____   _____   16. A Retail Information Systems Conference, held by the National Retail Federation, expressed the use of information technology as "Crunch data. Crunch numbers. Crunch the competition."

_____   _____   17. GS1 is an international non-profit association dedicated to the development and implementation of global standards and solutions for the efficiency of supply chains. The GS1 System has standards for bar codes, electronic messaging, synchronization of consistent data, and RFID technology to immediately track items.

_____   _____   18. "Compliance" is specified by many retailers, which requires all suppliers to use compatible technology through the entire soft goods chain. It has encouraged many companies to update their business practices.

_____   _____   19. "Very small aperture terminals" (VSAT) technology is based on satellite network communications, to transmit data, broadcast programs and meetings, send out retail news, communicate with business partners, etc.

_____   _____   20. Expo Scan Tech is a large, global exhibition showcasing solutions for the identification (ID) and automatic data capture (ADC) industries. Lately it has been held in Argentina.

The most interesting statement is #_____ because _____

_____

_____

_____

_____

_____

The Improving Textile/Apparel Industry

Activity D	**Name** _____
Chapter 5	**Date** _____ **Period**_____

Complete the following exercise.

1. Tell about UPC and EPC, and how they are used differently from each other. _____

    _____

    _____

2. What types of costs, quality, and trust existed in the past, when there were adversarial relationships between the segments of the textile-apparel industry? _____

    _____

    _____

3. What did U.S. business leaders from all parts of the textile/apparel pipeline decide could happen if all segments could cooperate to satisfy the final consumer? _____

    _____

    _____

4. What three entities benefit from the proactive policy of industry cooperation? _____

    _____

    _____

5. What do recorded product codes of merchandise being sold at retail through checkout scanners and computers trigger? _____

    _____

6. With Quick Response, what happens when apparel manufacturers run low on fabrics and sewing supplies? _____

    _____

    _____

7. With Quick Response, why are inventories kept lower and supply mistakes reduced? _____

    _____

    _____

8. Relate the old "push" method and new "pull" of Quick Response to the product-oriented and marketing-oriented approaches discussed in Chapter 3. _____

    _____

    _____

(Continued)

Name_____

9. What do the general benefits of Quick Response include? _____

_____

_____

10. What is the mission of the Textile/Clothing Technology Corporation [TC]²? _____

_____

_____

11. What is the National Textile Center (NTC) and, in general, what does it do? _____

_____

_____

12. What organization encourages American manufacturers to use "Made in USA" labels? _____

_____

_____

13. What are "green committees"? _____

_____

_____

14. What are some ways that recycled textiles are used? _____

_____

_____

Fashion Market Flash Cards

Activity E   **Name** _____

Chapter 5   **Date** _____ **Period**_____

Cut out the following cards along the printed lines and, with a classmate, go through them as flash cards. First show the other person the definition and have him or her guess the word. After both of you have done that, reverse the procedure and show the other person the word, for which the definition should be given by the other student.

Market Growth	**Market Share**
Market Segmentation	**Target Marketing**
Demographics	**Psychographics**

(Continued)

The part of the total market controlled by a firm, usually computed by sales and indicated as a percentage of total industry.	An increase in the size of the entire market, with more products sold and higher total dollars of sales.
Defining the specialized niche of the market to whom the company wants to make its greatest appeal.	Dividing the total market into smaller groups that contain similar characteristics.
Statistics that try to explain consumer behavior through such variables as lifestyle, values, attitudes, and self-concept.	Vital statistics of human populations concerning age, gender, race, education, religion, income, occupation, and geographic locations.

(Continued)

Market Research	**Qualitative**
Quantitative	**Virtual Reality (VR)**
Product Development	**Information Systems**

(Continued)

What (the kinds of things) people feel or want.	The process of systematically gathering and analyzing information relating to a particular market.
Computer generated "cyberspace" that stimulates the user's senses to create a perception of being in another environment.	How strongly people feel about or want things.
Computer components that work together by combining data and procedures toward a certain outcome.	Carrying a product idea through stages from initial conceptualization to actual appearance in the market.

(Continued)

Bar Codes	**Radio Frequency Identification (RFID)**
Computer Hardware	**Computer Software**
Open Systems	**Outsourcing**
Compliance	**B2B EC**

(Continued)

Wireless data collection done with "smart labels" and electronic product codes through airwaves.	Product codes with dark bars and white spaces of varying widths, used on merchandise tags for electronic data collection.
Electronic operating systems that tell the computer to do the required procedures.	Electronic equipment consisting of keyboards, monitors, and printers.
The hiring of independent specialists to do particular work, rather than using company employees.	Computer technology that enables components from different suppliers to be compatible with each other to be mixed and matched.
Business-to-business electronic commerce which connects companies via the Internet.	Companies following industry requirements and using unified product code standards that communicate the same "electronic language."

(Continued)

Electronic Data Interchange (EDI)	**Collaboration**
Quick Response (QR)	**Synergy**
Textile/Clothing Technology Corporation [TC]^2	**Environmental Sustainability**
Ethics	**Social Responsibility**

(Continued)

Working together in an endeavor, cooperating to assist each other.

The exchange of information and transactions through computer linkages between companies using an understood digital format.

Cooperative interaction of parts for a total effect that is greater than if the parts were added together separately.

An industry program that ties together the entire textile/apparel pipeline with product codes, EDI, and long-term partnerships.

Not harming the environment or depleting natural resources.

An industry organization that researches high-tech apparel production innovations and helps the industry implement them.

Going beyond what is legal, to do what helps society.

Moral principles or rules of conduct that distinguish right from wrong.

Textile Fibers and Yarns

Fiber Information

Activity A   **Name** _____

Chapter 6   **Date** _____ **Period**_____

Respond to the following questions and statements about fibers.

1. Describe the two major categories of natural fibers:

   a. _____

   b. _____

2. What makes the quality of natural fibers vary? _____

   _____

   _____

3. Processing for natural fibers includes various amounts of what five steps? _____

   _____

   _____

   _____

   _____

   _____

4. Name each of the four main natural fibers and the source of each. _____

   _____

   _____

   _____

   _____

5. What are cotton bolls? _____

6. Why is washing and drying of cotton items at high temperatures not recommended? _____

   _____

   _____

   _____

(Continued)

Name _____

7. What determines the quality of wool fibers? _____

    _____

    _____

8. What is the difference between pure wool, virgin wool, and 100 percent wool? _____

    _____

    _____

    _____

9. Approximately how much silk fiber is produced in the U.S.? _____

10. What is the world's oldest textile fiber? _____

11. What is ramie? _____

    _____

    _____

12. Name five specialty hair fibers.

    _____

    _____

    _____

    _____

    _____

13. Describe the two major sources of manufactured fibers:

    _____

    _____

14. Describe the three steps used to make all manufactured fibers.

    a. _____

        _____

    b. _____

        _____

    c. _____

        _____

15. When is a new category established for generic fibers? _____

    _____

    _____

(Continued)

Name_____

16. Why do companies give trade names to the specific fibers they manufacture and sell? _____

_____

_____

17. What is the advantage of heat-sensitive fibers that have a low melting point? _____

_____

_____

18. What are some disadvantages of nonabsorbent fibers? _____

_____

_____

19. Why is the manufacturing of the generic group, lyocell, heralded? _____

_____

_____

20. Why is recognition of manufactured fiber generic categories high among consumers? _____

_____

_____

21. Why must early planning of color and texture take place at the primary (raw material) level of the soft goods chain? _____

_____

_____

22. Why are fibers with different physical characteristics blended? _____

_____

_____

Associate with an Association

Activity B   **Name** _____

Chapter 6   **Date** _____ **Period**_____

Look up one of the many fiber or yarn trade associations in the library or on the Internet. Complete the following information sheet and share the information in an oral report to the class.

Name of association:

_____

Primary goal or purpose of the association:

_____

_____

_____

Membership requirements or qualifications:

_____

_____

_____

_____

Total membership:

_____

Association publications:

_____

_____

Annual meetings or conventions:

_____

_____

_____

Other interesting facts about the association:

_____

_____

_____

Merchandising with Fibers

Activity C

Name _____

Chapter 6

Date _____ **Period** _____

Complete the following exercise about how fibers can be merchandised according to their characteristics.

1. Mount pictures here from magazines, catalogs, or online that show two apparel items made from different natural fibers. Describe the characteristics of each fiber that make it good for that use.

a. _____

_____

_____

_____

_____

_____

_____

_____

_____

_____

_____

_____

_____

_____

b. _____

_____

_____

_____

_____

_____

_____

_____

_____

_____

_____

_____

_____

_____

_____

(Continued)

Name_____

2. Mount pictures here from magazines, catalogs, or online that show two apparel items made from different manufactured fibers. Describe the characteristics of each fiber that make it good for that use.

a. _____

_____

_____

_____

_____

_____

_____

_____

_____

_____

_____

_____

b. _____

_____

_____

_____

_____

_____

_____

_____

_____

_____

_____

_____

Textile Fiber and Yarn Review Match

Activity D   Name _____

Chapter 6   Date _____ Period_____

Match the following terms and definitions by placing the correct letter next to each number. (Complete the first and second lists separately.)

_____ 1. The soft, hairy coat of an animal.

_____ 2. Natural fibers of animal origin.

_____ 3. An area within a retail store that is stocked and operated by someone else.

_____ 4. People who breed and raise animals on fur farms or ranches.

_____ 5. Fine quality, tight, smooth wools made from long combed fibers.

_____ 6. Fibers from plant sources, such as cotton, linen, rayon, and acetate.

_____ 7. A manufacturer of fur items.

_____ 8. A fluffy feather undercoating of geese and ducks, used as a lightweight insulator in apparel.

_____ 9. Long, fine, continuous threads found naturally as silk.

_____ 10. Having the ability to take in moisture.

_____ 11. Able to spring back when crushed, stretched, or wrinkled.

_____ 12. A tough, flexible material made from animal hides.

_____ 13. Textile strands from plants and animals.

_____ 14. Retail selling of merchandise owned by the producer, for which the store receives a percentage of the sale price.

_____ 15. Natural cellulosic fiber from the stalk of the flax plant.

_____ 16. Places that contain sample fabrics for the upcoming fashion season.

_____ 17. The process of preserving animal hides to make leather.

_____ 18. Companies that "dress" fur pelts to make them soft, flexible, and more suitable for use in consumer products.

_____ 19. High quality "genuine leather" used in consumer products.

_____ 20. Short lengths of natural fibers, or cut filament fibers.

A. absorbent
B. cellulosic fibers
C. consignment selling
D. down
E. fabric libraries
F. filaments
G. fur
H. fur processors
I. furrier
J. leased department
K. leather
L. linen
M. natural fibers
N. pelt producers
O. protein fibers
P. resilient
Q. staple fibers
R. tanning
S. top grain leather
T. worsted fabrics

(Continued)

Name_____

_____ 1. Fibers processed with chemicals, heat, or special machinery for added visual surface characteristics.

_____ 2. Method of mechanically pulling and twisting staple fibers together to obtain a continuous length of yarns.

_____ 3. Manufactured fibers modified slightly (within their generic groups) during production, resulting in a change in the properties of the fiber.

_____ 4. Process that curls or waves manufactured fibers to give them elasticity and resiliency similar to natural fibers.

_____ 5. The creative, forward-thinking introduction of new ideas.

_____ 6. Yarns made by mechanically pulling and twisting staple fibers together into a continuous length.

_____ 7. Yarns with plies of different fibers.

_____ 8. Chain-like chemical structures of molecules from which many manufactured fibers are made.

_____ 9. Fibers that are created through technology and produced artificially from substances such as cellulose, petroleum, and chemicals.

_____ 10. Fiber thickness or diameter.

_____ 11. The dispersing of moisture through a given area, such as pulling body moisture to the fabric surface.

_____ 12. Identification of families of manufactured fibers, categorized according to similar chemical compositions.

_____ 13. Nozzle with many tiny holes through which liquid fiber-forming solutions are forced to form manufactured filaments.

_____ 14. A small-scale trial production facility that uses commercial factory methods.

_____ 15. Each strand of yarn in a ply yarn.

_____ 16. Staple fibers used without spinning to fill pillows, mattresses, sleeping bags, and comforters.

_____ 17. Convincing customers that they need a product before trying to sell it to them.

_____ 18. Process of drawing, twisting, and winding fibers into yarns.

_____ 19. Advertising done jointly with the costs shared.

_____ 20. Making multifilament yarns simultaneously with extrusion from the spinneret.

AA.   combination yarns
BB.   cooperative advertising
CC.   crimping
DD.   denier
EE.   fiberfill
FF.   generic groups
GG.   innovation
HH.   manufactured fibers
II.   mechanical spinning
JJ.   missionary selling
KK.   pilot plant
LL.   ply
MM. polymers
NN.   solution spinning
OO.   spinneret
PP.   spinning
QQ.   spun yarns
RR.   textured
SS.   variants
TT.   wicking

Textile Fabrics and Finishes

Basic Fabric Construction

Activity A   **Name** _____

Chapter 7   **Date** _____ **Period**_____

From a skein of knitting yarn, cut 80 pieces—each 2½ inches long. In each of these four boxes, tape the ends of 10 pieces to the left sides and tops as indicated. Then weave the yarns to create samples of the weaves named under each box.

Tape 10 ends
Tape 10 ends

Single Yarn Plain Weave

Tape 10 ends
Tape 10 ends

2 × 2 Basket Weave

Tape 10 ends
Tape 10 ends

Twill Weave

Tape 10 ends
Tape 10 ends

Satin Weave

(Continued)

Name_____

Mount fabric samples of a weft knit, a warp knit, and a nonwoven fabric in the appropriate boxes. After examining the samples, describe each fabric in detail.

Construction: Weft knit

Description:

_____

_____

_____

_____

_____

_____

_____

Construction: Warp knit

Description:

_____

_____

_____

_____

_____

_____

_____

Construction: Nonwoven

Description:

_____

_____

_____

_____

_____

_____

_____

Other Fabric Constructions

Activity B　　　　　**Name** _____

Chapter 7　　　　　　**Date** _____ **Period**_____

Obtain four fabric samples of unique constructions, such as lace, brocade, artificial suede, double-knit, pile, fleece, or quilted fabrics. Mount them in the boxes. Unravel a corner of each sample, if possible. Indicate the type of construction, whether the fabric has been dyed or printed, any obvious finishes, and other details you notice about each one.

1. _____

_____

_____

_____

_____

2. _____

_____

_____

_____

_____

3. _____

_____

_____

_____

4. _____

_____

_____

_____

Fabrics and Finishes Match

Activity C   **Name** _____

Chapter 7   **Date** _____ **Period** _____

Match the following terms and definitions by placing the correct letter next to each number.

_____ 1. Finishes that become part of fabrics through chemical reactions with the fibers.

_____ 2. A layer of fiber ends raised from a fabric surface.

_____ 3. Businesses that convert greige goods to finished fabrics and distribute those fabrics.

_____ 4. Product ratings according to suitability for specific end uses.

_____ 5. Surface design added to a fabric.

_____ 6. Method of giving color to fibers, yarns, fabrics, or garments with natural or synthetic solutions.

_____ 7. When more product has been made than was ordered by customers.

_____ 8. Consultants that foresee the colors, textures, and silhouettes to predict coming trends.

_____ 9. Process for adding color, pattern, or design to the surface of fabrics.

_____ 10. The direction of the lengthwise and crosswise yarns or threads in a woven fabric.

_____ 11. Product ratings according to levels of defects.

_____ 12. The way fabrics feel to the touch.

_____ 13. The strong lengthwise edge of fabrics that does not ravel.

_____ 14. A fabric construction method done by looping yarns together.

_____ 15. Commodity textiles made continuously each year, with little or no change.

_____ 16. Three-layer textiles with batting in the middle, usually held together by machine stitching.

_____ 17. Chemical process that removes color, impurities, or spots from fibers or fabrics.

_____ 18. Liaison individual or company that matches the needs of textile buyers and sellers.

_____ 19. Finishes applied to textiles using machines rather than being chemically applied.

A. applied design
B. bleaching
C. chemical finishes
D. colorfast
E. converters
F. dyeing
G. forecasting services
H. grain
I. hand
J. knitting
K. mechanical finishes
L. nap
M. nonwovens
N. novelty fabrics
O. overrun
P. performance standards
Q. pile fabrics
R. printing
S. quality standards
T. quilted fabrics
U. selvage
V. staple fabrics
W. structural design
X. textile broker
Y. true bias
Z. weaving

(Continued)

Name_____

_____ 20. When color in a fabric will not fade or change with laundering, dry cleaning, or time and use.

_____ 21. "Built-in" texture or interest to fabrics when they are manufactured.

_____ 22. Fabrics of a compact matted web of fibers, rather than being woven or knitted.

_____ 23. Grainline that runs exactly halfway between the lengthwise and crosswise grains of a fabric.

_____ 24. Fashion fabrics that change with style trends.

_____ 25. Procedure of interlacing two sets of yarns at right angles to each other.

_____ 26. Material with a surface effect of tufts, loops, or other projecting yarns.

Inform the Customers

Activity D   **Name** _____

Chapter 7   **Date** _____ **Period** _____

Make a list of four questions about fabrics that customers might ask an employee of a retail store that sells fashion goods. Also write out informative answers to those questions that would help the customers evaluate apparel items to buy. Then, with a partner, role-play in front of the class with one of you pretending to be the customer asking the questions, and the other being the salesperson answering them. You will have a total of eight questions/answers—four from each of you.

1. (Question): _____

    _____

    _____

    (Answer): _____

    _____

    _____

    _____

2. (Question): _____

    _____

    _____

    (Answer): _____

    _____

    _____

    _____

3. (Question): _____

    _____

    _____

    (Answer): _____

    _____

    _____

    _____

4. (Question): _____

    _____

    _____

    (Answer): _____

    _____

    _____

Textile Fabrics and Finishes Review

Activity E   **Name** _____

Chapter 7   **Date** _____ **Period** _____

After reviewing the chapter, respond to the following questions or statements.

1. List the two major forms of fabric design. _____

2. What are the two most common ways to construct apparel fabrics? _____

3. In what direction does bias grain run in fabrics? _____

4. What types of designs are woven on jacquard looms? _____

5. What region of the U.S. has the largest concentration of knitted fabric producers? _____

6. How do flat knitting machines accomplish full-fashioned shaping? _____

7. Describe sweater knits. _____

8. What is the fastest industrial method of making fashion fabrics? _____

9. What is the most familiar warp knit fabric? _____

10. Describe the grainline, stretch, raveling, and price level of nonwoven fabrics. _____

11. What are laces and nets? _____

12. In fabrics, what is bonding? _____

13. Why do converters usually not handle woolen/worsted fabrics, industrial fabrics, and knit goods?

14. Describe cross dyeing. _____

(Continued)

Name _____

15. Describe even and uneven plaids. _____

_____

_____

16. Why has rotary screen printing become widely used? _____

_____

17. Why is digital ink-jet printing of fabrics becoming popular? _____

_____

_____

18. What is the difference between finishes that are described by a word ending in "proof" and one ending in "resistant" or "repellent"? _____

_____

_____

19. What are the two main categories of finishing processes for fabrics? _____

_____

20. Define *quality*. _____

_____

21. What does the technology of fabric manufacturing involve? _____

_____

_____

22. What fashion decisions are involved in fabric manufacturing? _____

_____

_____

_____

23. Are staple fabrics and novelty fabrics imported from other countries or made in the U.S. respectively?

_____

_____

24. What is meant when it is said that the textile segment is moving from a labor-intensive industry to a capital-intensive one? (Use the text glossary if necessary.) _____

_____

_____

_____

25. What fiber is predicted to dominate in the future, what characteristic type of yarns will gain popularity, and what fabric production method will increase? _____

_____

Using Design in *Fashion*

Going Deeper with Color

Activity A

Chapter 8

Name _____

Date _____ Period_____

Identify each color scheme shaded in these color wheels, name the colors used in each, and describe the color scheme. Then complete the activities on the back of this page.

1. Color scheme: _____

   Colors used: _____

   Statement: _____

   _____

   _____

2. Color scheme: _____

   Colors used: _____

   Statement: _____

   _____

   _____

3. Color scheme: _____

   Colors used: _____

   Statement: _____

   _____

   _____

4. Color scheme: _____

   Colors used: _____

   Statement: _____

   _____

   _____

(Continued)

79

Name _____

5. Color scheme: _____

   Colors used: _____

   Statement: _____

   _____

   _____

6. Color scheme: _____

   Colors used: _____

   Statement: _____

   _____

   _____

In items 7-13, place the letter of the best answer in the blank to the left of the description.

_____ 7. Best for people with quiet, shy personalities.

_____ 8. Best for dramatic, energetic, outgoing people.

_____ 9. Colors that represent water and the sky.

_____ 10. Ways that colors can effectively be used together.

_____ 11. Makes colors seem more exciting because they look brighter.

_____ 12. Makes a person look thinner and taller.

_____ 13. Colors that give a feeling of gaiety, activity, and cheerfulness.

A. bright colors
B. color schemes
C. pale, cool colors
D. single color outfit
E. extreme contrast
F. warm colors
G. cool colors

14. Describe the effects warm colors and cool colors can have in wearing apparel. _____

_____

_____

_____

15. Study current fashion magazines and catalogs to determine the "color story" for this fashion season. Report your findings here, and express any thoughts you have about the use of these colors in the latest apparel being offered to consumers. _____

_____

_____

_____

_____

_____

_____

Define and Draw the Line

Activity B   **Name** _____

Chapter 8   **Date** _____ **Period** _____

Define each term, briefly describing the effect each type of line has in apparel, and draw an example of each where a box is provided.

1. Horizontal lines:

    _____

    _____

    _____

    _____

    _____

2. Vertical lines:

    _____

    _____

    _____

    _____

    _____

3. Jagged lines:

    _____

    _____

    _____

    _____

    _____

4. Diagonal lines:

    _____

    _____

    _____

    _____

    _____

(Continued)

Name_____

5. Straight lines:

_____

_____

_____

_____

_____

6. Curved lines:

_____

_____

_____

_____

_____

7. Structural lines:

_____

_____

_____

_____

_____

8. Decorative lines:

_____

_____

_____

_____

_____

Shape and Texture

Activity C   **Name** _____

Chapter 8   **Date** _____ **Period**_____

Complete the following exercises about shape and texture.

1. Find a picture of a fashionable outfit with an interesting shape and mount it in the box. Describe the outfit's overall silhouette and explain how it would flatter or be unflattering, or disguise various parts of the human body.

_____

_____

_____

_____

_____

_____

_____

_____

_____

_____

_____

_____

_____

_____

_____

_____

_____

_____

_____

_____

_____

_____

_____

_____

_____

_____

(Continued)

Name_____

2. List six different words that describe various textures.

_____

_____

_____

_____

_____

_____

3. Why would the same hue look different in satin than it would in corduroy or gabardine?

_____

_____

4. Gather and mount three fabric samples with different textures in these boxes. On the lines, identify the texture as structural or added visual texture. Then describe the texture and explain the effects or illusions that could be created by use of that texture in apparel.

a. Type of texture: _____

Description: _____

Effects of the texture in apparel: _____

_____

_____

_____

_____

b. Type of texture: _____

Description: _____

Effects of the texture in apparel: _____

_____

_____

_____

_____

c. Type of texture: _____

Description: _____

Effects of the texture in apparel: _____

_____

_____

_____

_____

The Design Principles

Activity D

Chapter 8

Name _____

Date _____ Period_____

Complete the following exercises about design principles.

1. What does balance imply as a principle of design? _____

_____

2. What type of balance is shown here in figure a?

_____

3. Name the other kind of balance. Draw a design that shows it on the form provided in figure b.

_____

a.

b.

4. Describe the proportion of the parts of the design in figure c in relation to the other parts and to the wearer.

_____

_____

_____

_____

_____

_____

c.

d.

5. Explain where emphasis is used in the design in figure d, and what it achieves.

_____

_____

_____

_____

_____

_____

(Continued)

Name_____

e.   f.   g.

6. Name and describe the type of rhythm that is represented by the design in figure e. _____

_____

_____

7. Name and describe the type of rhythm that is represented by the design in figure f. _____

_____

_____

8. Describe repetition as a type of rhythm. Then draw a design that shows repetition on figure g.

_____

_____

9. After the principles of design have been used as the guidelines for combining the elements of design, what one word describes the goal of what should have been achieved? _____

Relating to Design

Activity E   **Name** _____

Chapter 8   **Date** _____ **Period**_____

For each category listed on the left (#1-4), circle the word or phrase among the rest that does not fit.
Then, on the line directly underneath, add one more word or phrase that does fit into that category.
Then, pretend to be a wardrobe consultant or retail salesperson, and give sound advice to each of the
people in #5-10.

1. To look taller and thinner:	one-color outfits	smooth, flat texture	horizontal lines	simple, uncluttered look
_____				
2. To look shorter and wider:	bulky, heavy textures	narrow silhouettes	bold prints and plaids	emphasis leading the eye down
_____				
3. To attract attention to areas:	cool hues	shiny textures	large, busy prints	clingy fabrics
_____				
4. To avoid attention to areas:	soft fabrics	light, bright colors	flat, dull textures	plain, unpatterned fabrics
_____				

5. Mrs. Smith has a petite figure and is considering two different dresses. One has a bright, wide belt
   at the waist and fabric with a large design. The other has a thin, matching belt and fabric with a
   small design. Which dress would you recommend to Mrs. Smith and why? _____

   _____

   _____

   _____

6. Mr. Adams is very tall and has a slim build. He has been wearing one-color suits to work, but feels
   he looks like a "string bean." His workplace is now encouraging more casual attire. Mr. Adams
   likes shirts, sweaters, and slacks but needs general advice about silhouettes, color combinations,
   textures, etc. What advice would you give him? _____

   _____

   _____

   _____

(Continued)

Name _____

7. Keona Johnson wears size 14 blouses because she has wide shoulders. However, her hips are small so she wears a size 10 in skirts and slacks. How would you help her not to look top-heavy?

_____

_____

8. Mrs. Cohen is quite short, and is heavier than most of her friends. She wants to get a new sweater and pair of pants to wear to a casual get-together, but is unsure about what would make her look taller and more slender. She is looking at bulky sweaters in bright colors, and tight pants. Can you advise her if these are the best choices? If not, what should she choose? _____

_____

_____

_____

9. Matt is short and slender, which makes him look younger than his age of 16 years. For his upcoming job interview at a local restaurant, he wants to look bigger, to seem older and more responsible. How can he use the elements and principles of design to maximize his appearance goal?

_____

_____

_____

_____

10. Mrs. King has a good facial complexion, a nice smile, and attractive eyes, but does not like the shape of her body. For her nephew's wedding, she is considering buying either a deep blue dress in a soft, unpatterned crepe with a white ruffled collar or a yellow satin dress with rows of contrasting lace attractively placed at intervals around the skirt. Which dress would you recommend to Mrs. King and why? _____

_____

_____

_____

Designer Myths or Truths

Activity A   Name _____

Chapter 9   Date _____ Period _____

After reading each of the following statements, indicate if you think the statement is a myth or a truth by checking the appropriate column. Then turn to the back of this page to check your answers. Later, discuss the statements as a class.

	Myth	Truth
1. The one characteristically American style of dress to develop in the 20th century was sportswear.		
2. Christian Dior became the "father of Paris couture" as the first French high fashion designer in 1938.		
3. Like all design trends, fashion colors and accessory styles go through cycles that include introduction, rise to widespread acceptance, decline, and disappearance.		
4. "Vendeuse" is the term for French ready-to-wear designers.		
5. U.S. fashion designer, Anne Klein, is credited with originating the "American look" of sporty, casual, and comfortable clothing with functional designs.		
6. American high fashion designer, Pauline Trigere, had cutting shears that were custom-molded to the shape of her fingers. She directly cut out designs that were in her head, saying that she was bad at sketching.		
7. High fashion designers have enlarged their workrooms so their RTW lines can be manufactured there as well as their designer lines.		
8. Logos are a very important part of each designer's image-building process. Designers try to determine just the right look to set their logo apart from others, as well as deciding on its size and placement on their goods.		
9. Little-known custom designers can be found in many cities. They do work for special clients, with individual fabric selections and custom styling and fit.		
10. Chambre Syndicale de la Couture trade association subgroups represent French ready-to-wear designers and labels.		
11. The emergence of the working woman is probably the single most powerful influence on womenswear fashions today, while casual workdays have been a boon to men's fashions.		
12. The fashion industries of most countries stage week-long trade shows twice a year (spring and fall) with showings that are attended by retail buyers, celebrities, and the fashion press.		

(Continued)

Name_____

1. *Truth.* America developed casual lifestyles that required functional apparel for recreational activities, car travel, and leisure relaxation.

2. *Myth.* Charles Frederick Worth, a British designer who opened the first couture house in Paris in 1858, is generally regarded as the "father of Paris couture."

3. *Truth.* Fashion colors and accessories cycle over time, just as garment designs do. Also, ideas in home furnishings, buildings, artwork, cars, foods, leisure, pastimes, and other arts and activities go through cycles of varying lengths of time.

4. *Myth.* "Vendeuse" is the term for a French salesperson. "Createurs" are French ready-to-wear designers.

5. *Myth.* Claire McCardell designed a travel wardrobe in 1934 consisting of jersey knit separates that could be mixed and matched in different ways to combine for almost any activity. She also introduced large pockets, trouser pleats, top-stitching, rivets, and denim for women's apparel.

6. *Truth.* Creative designers have their own ways of doing their craft. Although it is expensive to cut right into fine fabrics, rather than sketching ideas as most other designers do, Pauline Trigere had the skill and confidence developed over many decades of creating womenswear. She had been in the business since 1942 and designed "Gold Violin" fashions for seniors.

7. *Myth.* Ready-to-wear lines are manufactured in factories apart from the workrooms that produce couture designs. In fact, they are often made in other parts of the world, such as Asia. The company, GFT S.p.A., is an Italian clothing producer that often manufactures Armani, Valentino, Ungaro, Dior, and other designer labels.

8. *Truth.* Decisions about the logo and image are not taken lightly. Design firms spend large amounts of money and many hours of deliberation considering the specifics of their logo, to portray the right message.

9. *Truth.* These "high-class dressmaking shops" are owned by creative people who do not have the desire, important contacts, or financial backing needed to grow into major fashion names.

10. *Truth.* The Chambre Syndicale du Prêt-à-Porter is a subgroup with members who qualify if they have similar brand name recognition and prestige as couturiers. The Federation Francaise du Prêt-à-Porter Feminim is an organization for companies that mass-produce RTW women's fashions.

11. *Truth.* Not only are more women in the workforce, but more are professionals with higher levels of responsibility and wardrobe needs. This has raised the sales of labels such as Liz Claiborne and Donna Karan. Correspondingly, more relaxed office wardrobes have sparked the most interest in men's fashions ever recorded.

12. *Truth.* The trade shows are well organized with many collection showings scheduled in a shared central location.

Designer Trade Aspects

Activity B   Name _____

Chapter 9   Date _____ Period_____

Read the following statements. Place a check if you think the statement is an interesting aspect of the fashion design segment, or if it seems uninteresting to you. You will not be graded on your responses. Then choose what you feel the most interesting statement of the group is and explain your reaction to it in detail.

Interesting   Uninteresting

_____   _____   1. Some fashion designers are so well-known that they can use just their first name for their secondary line. Examples are the secondary lines "Michael" (Michael Kors), "Karl" (Karl Lagerfeld), and "Marc" (Marc Jacobs).

_____   _____   2. An intern for Yves Saint Laurent and other design houses in Paris learned to handcraft beautiful garments that sold for thousands of dollars. Then he started his own business, in the U.S., designing budget-priced, mass-produced women's clothes. The low-priced market has large demand, while the expensive market has small demand plus many designers selling in it.

_____   _____   3. Recently, menswear designers have been designing womenswear lines and womenswear designers have branched out to do menswear lines. The types of garments for men and women have become more similar, so the same skills can be used to design and manufacture both.

_____   _____   4. Fashion events in major market centers are listed in the Fashion Calendar, which informs industry insiders about market weeks and collection showings. It serves as a clearinghouse for dates and information about key national and international fashion events.

_____   _____   5. About 60 New York fashion designers who are CFDA members hold their showings to retail buyers and the press through "7th on Sixth, Inc." It is a not-for-profit company that organizes shows in Manhattan.

_____   _____   6. Extravaganzas called "7th on Sale" have sold designer fashions in New York and San Francisco at bargain prices to raise money for AIDS and HIV programs. Merchandise was donated by industry participants, and thousands of volunteers participated. Other sales have benefited breast cancer research.

_____   _____   7. Fashion pirates have posted high quality photos of the collections of about 100 top designers on the Internet within a day of the showings. This enables quickie knockoffs to be stitched up and on the market before the designer goods hit the stores. Designers are investigating legal retaliation.

_____   _____   8. Los Angeles fashion is influenced by different ethnic and income groups, for example, beach vs. Hollywood wear; or hippies, groupies, and yuppies. Tipped off-kilter, designs can look cheap and gaudy. However, just the right blend yields strangely beautiful, oddly hip, eclectic, unmistakably fantastic L.A. chic.

(Continued)

Name_____

Interesting   Uninteresting

_____   _____   9. Drawing up seating charts at collection showings is ticklish business. Influential editors of the top fashion magazines, buyers from the best stores, and celebrity guests get top priority. Others are placed farther back according to a pecking order, and still others are relegated to viewing dress rehearsals!

_____   _____   10. Since the number of handsewn-to-order "haute couture" designers that meet French government requirements for that designation has dwindled in number, some designers are now using the term "semi-couture" to describe machine-made clothes in tiny quantities of fine materials. This is called "demi-couture" in French.

The most interesting statement is #_____ because _____

_____

_____

_____

_____

_____

_____

_____

_____

_____

_____

_____

What's the Difference?

Activity C   **Name** _____

Chapter 9   **Date** _____ **Period**_____

In relation to this chapter, what is the difference between:

1. Couture and bridge lines? _____

   _____

   _____

2. Moderate and budget (price market categories of apparel)? _____

   _____

   _____

3. Custom-made and ready-to-wear? _____

   _____

   _____

4. Adaptation and knockoff? _____

   _____

   _____

5. Margin and perceived difference? _____

   _____

   _____

6. Collection and line? _____

   _____

   _____

7. Licensing and franchising? _____

   _____

   _____

8. Franchisor and franchisee? _____

   _____

   _____

9. House boutiques and designer patterns? _____

   _____

   _____

(Continued)

Name _____

10. Prophetic fashions and electronic graphics interchange? _____

_____

_____

11. Design stylist and couturier? _____

_____

_____

12. Logo and caution? _____

_____

_____

13. Haute couture and alta moda? _____

_____

_____

14. Chambre Syndicale de la Couture and Council of Fashion Designers of America? _____

_____

_____

15. Fashion piracy and prêt-à-porter? _____

_____

_____

Fashion Design Segment Review

Activity D   **Name** _____

Chapter 9   **Date** _____ **Period** _____

After reviewing the chapter, answer the following questions.

1. What traditional action is taken by name designers at the end of their collection showings? _____

   _____

   _____

2. Name the contributing factors to the high costs of couture showings. _____

   _____

   _____

3. At what time of the year are the major ready-to-wear collections shown? _____

   _____

   _____

4. How are orderly times arranged for all the designers to be able to show their lines? _____

   _____

   _____

5. Give at least three reasons why consumers no longer buy couture fashions.

   _____

   _____

   _____

6. If couture collections lose money, why do designers continue to have them? _____

   _____

   _____

7. What disadvantage of licensing do designers have to guard against? _____

   _____

   _____

8. What do license directors and design studios do? _____

   _____

   _____

9. What two entities must franchisors satisfy to continue demand for their franchise? _____

   _____

   _____

(Continued)

Name_____

10. How far ahead of the consumer buying time do RTW designers start work on their company's lines? _____

_____

11. In fashion, what are "winners"? _____

_____

_____

12. Why are costly mistakes avoided by CAD? _____

_____

_____

13. What country has led world fashion for hundreds of years? _____

14. What were the general purposes for the formation of the Chambre Syndicale de la Couture?

_____

_____

15. Name three of the activities/responsibilities of the Chambre Syndicale de la Couture.

_____

_____

_____

16. At couture showings, why are RTW trade buyers charged more for individual garments than private customers are charged? _____

_____

_____

17. Why are the countries of Central and South America good sources of supply for U.S. retail buyers?

_____

_____

18. What part of China is the world's largest exporter of fashion apparel? _____

_____

19. What organization presents the most important current U.S. fashion awards? _____

_____

20. What is the U.S. fashion industry's highest honor today? _____

_____

Fashion Design Quiz

Activity E　　　　　　　**Name** _____

Chapter 9　　　　　　　　**Date** _____　**Period**_____

Write one true/false question for each of the chapter sections noted, and write the correct answers on another piece of paper. If your question is false, write the sentence as a true statement on your other piece of paper. Then exchange quizzes with a classmate to try to answer each other's questions correctly on this page. Check answers with the prepared answer sheet.

True or False

Price Market Categories of Apparel—(through bridge):

_____ 1.　_____

　　　　　　　_____

　　　　　　　_____

　　　　　　　_____

Price Market Categories of Apparel—(better through budget):

_____ 2.　_____

　　　　　　　_____

　　　　　　　_____

　　　　　　　_____

Collection Showings:

_____ 3.　_____

　　　　　　　_____

　　　　　　　_____

　　　　　　　_____

Capitalizing on Name Recognition—(through house boutiques):

_____ 4.　_____

　　　　　　　_____

　　　　　　　_____

　　　　　　　_____

Capitalizing on Name Recognition—(licensing through sewing patterns):

_____ 5.　_____

　　　　　　　_____

　　　　　　　_____

　　　　　　　_____

(Continued)

Name _____

The Designing Process—(through sources of inspiration):

_____ 6. _____

_____

_____

_____

The Designing Process—(using technology in fashion design):

_____ 7. _____

_____

_____

_____

World Fashion Design Centers—(through European fashion centers):

_____ 8. _____

_____

_____

_____

World Fashion Design Centers—(Canada through other world locations):

_____ 9. _____

_____

_____

_____

U.S. Fashion Awards and Associations:

_____ 10. _____

_____

_____

_____

Ready-to-Wear Manufacturing

Expanding Your Ready-to-Wear Knowledge

Activity A   **Name** _____

Chapter 10   **Date** _____ **Period**_____

Complete this exercise. Then use it as a basis for class discussion.

1. Describe, in detail, the **conversion process** that takes place during apparel production. _____

    _____

    _____

    _____

2. Even though the equation is **productivity = output/employee hours**, it would be difficult to compare the productivity of one worker who assembles 15 suit collars in one hour (stitch, trim, and turn) against another worker who sews 40 patch pockets onto a jacket in one hour (place and stitch). Thus, why do you think productivity numbers are usually compared over time for the same operation? _____

    _____

3. Look up **variable costs** and **fixed costs** in the glossary and write the definitions here. _____

    _____

    _____

    _____

4. By substituting the word "production" for the word "sales" in both definitions above, relate those two types of costs to chart 10-13 of the textbook. _____

    _____

    _____

5. From studying chart 10-13, write definitions in your own words for the terms **direct labor** and **indirect labor**. _____

    _____

    _____

6. If materials, labor, and overhead costs increase, what happens to the amount of **profit**? _____

    _____

    _____

(Continued)

Name _____

7. If the **costing structure** of a firm shows the **percentages** of expenses for materials, labor, overhead, and other needs, what column in chart 10-13 shows the costing structure of a typical apparel manufacturing company? _____

_____

8. Look up the meaning of **percentage** in the glossary. Then consider that, if costs for producing a line total 100%, why can the **costing structure** of a large firm be similar to that of a small firm?

_____

_____

9. After re-reading the chapter section about apparel firms using contractors for their manufacturing, try to relate those same advantages to using innovative production technology. _____

_____

_____

_____

10. How do you feel about the arrangement where workers receive their **pay** according to how many times they have quickly accomplished the same task (individual incentive; progressive bundle system)? _____

_____

11. How do you feel about the arrangement where workers receive their **pay** according to the performance of an entire team made up of several different people, with the option of bonuses for high group performance (team incentive; modular manufacturing)? _____

_____

_____

_____

12. When apparel items are manufactured in remote locations far away, **lead and response times** can be very long. Discuss a situation in which the factory has to order and receive their fabric from a great distance, train unskilled workers to do the sewing procedures, get the right labels and tags in a different language from their own, pack the goods properly for shipping, and send them a long distance to their destination. _____

_____

_____

_____

_____

_____

_____

_____

Manufacturing Business Team

Activity B **Name** _____

Chapter 10 **Date** _____ **Period** _____

Form an "apparel manufacturing business team" with a group of classmates. After considering the following questions, give your company a name and describe your business in detail to the rest of the class. Tell why you made each decision for your business.

Names of students on your apparel manufacturing business team: _____

_____

_____

Size of firm (large = many divisions; medium = a few divisions; small = one product line): _____

_____

_____

Type of apparel line(s) (men's casual sportswear, bridal/formal, women's career, etc.): _____

_____

_____

Target market and general price level category: _____

_____

_____

Degree of automation versus labor: _____

_____

_____

_____

_____

Manufacturing plans—inside or outside shop: _____

_____

_____

_____

_____

Production location (domestic, offshore, specific region, etc.): _____

_____

_____

(Continued)

Name _____

Plans for use of profits (new equipment, market research, product development, employee bonuses, hire more employees, stockholder dividends, other?): _____

_____

_____

_____

_____

_____

Competitive strategy to pursue: _____

_____

_____

_____

_____

_____

What **fashion/production seasons** should be included? _____

_____

_____

_____

Name of the company: _____

Create a Fashion Apparel Line

Activity C   **Name** _____

Chapter 10   **Date** _____ **Period**_____

Pretend you are creating a fashion apparel line. Answer the following questions about your fashion apparel line.

1. The line will be aimed at which sex (menswear, womenswear, unisex)? _____

   _____

2. The line will be part of what price/style market (bridge, moderate, budget, etc.)? _____

   _____

3. What competitive approach will be used (low-cost, differentiation, narrow market niche)?

   _____

4. What article categories will be included (suits, coats, shoes, mix-and-match separates, etc.)?

   _____

5. Your market will include what age groups and/or size ranges (infants, teens, adults, tall, etc.)?

   _____

6. The line will be sold in what geographical areas (sunbelt, snowbelt, nationwide, worldwide)?

   _____

7. What will be the general location of production (domestic, Western Hemisphere, Asia, etc.)?

   _____

8. How much manufacturing will be done "in-house" and how much will be contracted out?

   _____

9. What type of fabrication will be used (lightweight, heavyweight, knits, wovens, leather, etc.)?

   _____

10. What production seasons will be included (spring, fall, holiday, etc.)? _____

   _____

Describe your line for one fashion season, including any special features that give it a market advantage.

_____

_____

_____

_____

_____

Manufacturing Crossword

Activity D   **Name** _____

Chapter 10   **Date** _____ **Period** _____

Complete this crossword puzzle using the clues listed.

Name_____

Across

1. An _____ shop is an apparel firm that uses contractors to do everything but the sewing, and sometimes the cutting.
4. Independently-owned sewing factories that produce goods for apparel firms.
9. The _____ of production include resources, labor, capital, and business leadership.
10. All sewing tasks are done by a single operator in the _____ system of garment manufacturing.
11. The transformation of resources into a form that people need or want.
14. Apparel manufacturing companies are commonly referred to as _____.
15. The apparel industry is often called the _____ trade.
16. _____ work assigns one specific task to each person along an assembly line.
19. A _____ district is an area within a fashion city where most of the apparel companies are located.
21. Materials for the functional parts of garments, such as linings, zippers, hooks, snaps, thread, and labels.
23. Human engineering that matches human performance to the tasks performed, the equipment used, and the environment.
28. To send commercial products out of a country to other countries.
29. All members of a group share in extra incentive rewards when the group exceeds work expectations.
30. An _____ shop is an apparel firm that does all stages of garment production itself, from design concept and fabric purchasing, through all sewing procedures, to the shipment of finished garments.
32. Work _____ is the ergonomic matching of jobs and equipment to employees, the company's output requirements, compensation plans, and worker behaviors that are reinforced.
33. _____ sourcing is buying goods from overseas producers, or contracting with foreign manufacturing plants.
34. Sourcing _____ are experts hired to guide companies to identify countries and factories that give the best opportunities for their apparel production.

Down

2. A _____ production system is a CAM piecework system with an overhead product-carrier that moves cut garment pieces through the production line.
3. Apparel _____ are outside shops that never produce any of their own goods.
5. The use of machinery to perform physical tasks that are normally performed by humans.
6. _____ manufacturing divides production employees into independent module work groups that sort out problems and agree on their own work assignments and schedules.
7. The progressive _____ system of apparel manufacturing moves packages of cut garment parts, in dozens, through the sewing line—from station to station.
8. A measure of how efficiently or effectively resources are used, calculated by dividing output by employee hours spent achieving that output.
12. _____ time is how long it takes to produce and deliver merchandise after it has been ordered.
13. The apparel industry is made up of many various _____ trades.
17. Fabrics, leathers, furs, or other materials used in making fashion goods.
18. Fashion _____ are distinct retail selling periods.
20. Modular manufacturing is sometimes also referred to as _____ manufacturing.
22. New York's _____ Avenue is where designers' showrooms and apparel industry company offices are located.
24. Goods that come into the country from foreign sources.
25. The seeking of vendors or producers of desired goods.
26. _____ time is the amount of time between placing an order for merchandise and the desired delivery date.
27. The decorative materials of fashion items, such as buttons, laces, belts, and braids that are added to enhance the design.
31. _____ production is the manufacturing of goods in one's own country.

Wholesale Apparel Marketing and Distribution

Wholesale Apparel Marketing Facts

Activity A

Chapter 11

Name _____

Date _____ Period_____

The statements included in this activity relate to wholesale apparel marketing facts. To the left of each statement, place a "+" if it is true and an "o" if it is false. Correct each false statement by writing it as a true statement, with supporting information, on the following page.

True (+) or False (o)

_____ 1. The inventories of manufacturers and retailers are basically the same.

_____ 2. It is expensive for companies to keep large or wrong inventories.

_____ 3. Materials handling activities consume most of the time from product beginning to completion.

_____ 4. Computerized production applications have not been able to improve materials handling problems.

_____ 5. With product lifestyle management (PLM), computerized manufacturing methods show when and what materials are put into products as soon as they are used.

_____ 6. If done well, just-in-time inventory systems eliminate waste by utilizing small inventories that require less storage space, accounting, and investment.

_____ 7. Consolidated shipping is a practice of unloading goods from an incoming shipment directly onto outbound trucks and cross-docking is when two or more shippers put together a truckload, which lowers transportation costs.

_____ 8. Inventory control is one of the primary competitive advantages that U.S.-based manufacturers can use to combat imports.

_____ 9. Benchmarking results in change that brings about better processes.

_____ 10. American business has discovered that improved quality is an expense that reduces profits.

_____ 11. Total quality management (TQM) encompasses the concepts of empowerment of employees, work teams, and benchmarking.

_____ 12. The increased staff sizes of many companies make it critical that each employee's work be superior and valued.

_____ 13. A distinctive trademark can support a company's reputation of quality and style, providing consumers with a sense of purchasing confidence.

_____ 14. Federal registration of trademarks gives companies exclusive ownership and privilege to use the marks, and to sue in federal court for trademark infringement.

(Continued)

Name_____

_____ 15. Challenging trademark counterfeiters in court can remove counterfeiters from the market, minimize damage to the company's reputation, and deter other companies from trademark infringement.

_____ 16. Computerized machines for apparel manufacturing are being used more universally now because the price is coming down, the systems are more user friendly, and there is a larger pool of technology-literate workers to operate them.

_____ 17. The best application for robotics is doing unusual, one-of-a-kind procedures.

_____ 18. The main advantage of computer-integrated manufacturing (CIM) is that it allows maximum coordination and centralized control of production operations.

Statement Numbers	Corrected Statements
_____	
_____	
_____	
_____	
_____	
_____	

Apparel Sales and Distribution

Activity B   **Name** _____

Chapter 11   **Date** _____ **Period**_____

Complete the following activity about apparel sales and distribution.

1. List the advantages of apparel being sold directly from producer to retailer, with no wholesale
   segment in between. _____

   _____

   _____

   _____

   _____

2. Explain why many apparel firms have permanent leased showrooms in marts. _____

   _____

   _____

   _____

   _____

3. Explain why apparel manufacturers that sell their lines to consumers online may cause problems
   for themselves. _____

   _____

   _____

   _____

   _____

4. Describe what apparel company sales reps do after market weeks. _____

   _____

   _____

   _____

   _____

5. Explain what sales managers do and what independent sales reps sell. _____

   _____

   _____

   _____

   _____

(Continued)

Name _____

6. Describe the selling aids that manufacturers sometimes provide to retailers. _____

_____

_____

_____

_____

7. List the advantages of trunk shows for customers, manufacturers, and retailers. _____

_____

_____

_____

_____

8. Explain the importance of standardized shipping container markings. _____

_____

_____

_____

_____

9. Describe how satellite shipment tracking is enabling freight carriers, such as highway trucks, to be part of the electronic linkage pipeline. _____

_____

_____

_____

10. Explain why some companies outsource their physical distribution to third-party experts. _____

_____

_____

_____

_____

11. Describe the probable smaller and more dynamic distribution facilities of the future. _____

_____

_____

_____

12. Explain the goal of the American Apparel and Footwear Association. _____

_____

_____

Apparel Business Responses

Activity C   **Name** _____

Chapter 11   **Date** _____ **Period** _____

Write your thoughts about the following statements on the lines provided. Then share your thoughts with others by having a class discussion of each situation described. Also notice the terms (in bold print) that are currently being used in the industry.

1. Since most of a clothing production operator's time is spent **accepting**, **aligning**, and **transferring** the work (rather than sewing), more and more firms are supplementing traditional operations with robots, vision systems, computer-controlled conveyors, and stitchless joining. _____

    _____

    _____

    _____

    _____

2. If flaws or mistakes are found in garments at the end of production, the items are either returned to the operator responsible to be fixed or sold cheaply as seconds (a reactive approach). The **proactive** approach of taking a bit more time and care to make items perfect the first time saves overall time, money, and customer satisfaction. _____

    _____

    _____

    _____

    _____

3. Companies don't often hear about a consumer who buys their product and is disappointed by poor quality. It has been said that for every customer who buys a **defective product**, many more sales are lost because of friends telling friends. Also, it costs about five times more to get a new customer as it does to keep the customers a company already has. _____

    _____

    _____

    _____

    _____

4. An old saying is, "If it ain't broke, don't fix it." However, with an emphasis on **benchmarking** for quality products, the new saying is, "If it's working well, find a way to make it work better, because if you don't, somebody else will." _____

    _____

    _____

    _____

    _____

(Continued)

Name _____

5. The apparel production segment of the pipeline has a tendency toward **overcapacity**, or producing more merchandise than the market can absorb. This **oversaturation** of available goods creates intense competition for sales to retailers. _____

_____

_____

_____

6. Apparel companies have their own production calendars, with new lines out at specified times that also coordinate with market selling weeks. For instance, **line breaks** of the upscale Girbaud fashions are six times a year, with two delivery periods within each break. _____

_____

_____

_____

7. Automation for speed and efficiency of the materials handling aspect of production, for a faster manufacturing **cycle time** (also called **throughput**), is crucial to improving the profitability of apparel firms. _____

_____

_____

_____

8. CAD, CAM, and CIM are also helping to sell lines to retailers through **audio/visual sales presentations**. They have music, text, graphics, and garment drawings projected onto large screens in showroom theaters. The sales content comes directly out of the design and manufacturing technology. _____

_____

_____

_____

9. Computer technology does **texture mapping** so well these days, that when different fabrics are electronically substituted onto the same garment design, the computer images on the screen show the proper grain, shading, and textures of the new fabrics for the fashions. _____

_____

_____

_____

10. To use logistics as a competitive advantage, apparel companies are **trading off**. They are spending more money in the area of fast, correct deliveries to stores, to achieve overall better service and higher eventual profits. _____

_____

_____

_____

(Continued)

Name_____

11. **Pool distribution** involves using the services of a distribution company that others also use. Many apparel companies are now contracting with regional **break bulk operators** who receive large truckload quantities of goods that they quickly sort and deliver to individual stores. _____

_____

_____

_____

12. The type of logistics a company requires depends on how many **demand points** (stores or delivery addresses) their goods must go to in each area, and if each destination will receive small (less-than-truckload) or large shipments. _____

_____

_____

_____

13. **Extranets** are private computer networks within organizations that provide access to trading partners for checking on shipment status, product availability for forecasts and production planning, etc. They involve encrypted transactions and various levels of authorization. _____

_____

_____

_____

14. **Speech (voice) recognition** systems have many uses in warehouses and distribution centers. Workers wear a headset with microphone to do manufacturing inspection, picking/packing, package sorting, receiving, returns processing, and inventory control jobs with their hands free to do coordinating work. _____

_____

_____

_____

15. The need to place inventory in storage is eliminated with **cross-docking**. One example of this distribution approach is pre-packing merchandise for individual stores of chains and moving the goods directly from the receiving dock at the distribution center to the shipping dock. _____

_____

_____

_____

16. Shipping by more than one different type of equipment, for savings or speed, is called **intermodal transport**. Long-distance rail transport of truck trailers might be followed by over-the-road delivery by truck. _____

_____

_____

_____

Fashion Market Match

Activity D   Name _____

Chapter 11   Date _____ Period_____

Match the following terms and definitions by placing the correct letter next to each number.

_____ 1. Bringing into a store a designer's/producer's collection of samples for a limited time, to take orders from customers for later delivery.

_____ 2. Predicting the quantity of each item that will be sold during a particular future fiscal time period.

_____ 3. The national trade association representing U.S. apparel, footwear, and other sewn products and companies.

_____ 4. The selling and shipping of goods to anyone who can pay for the merchandise.

_____ 5. The process of maintaining inventories at a level that prevents stockouts and minimizes holding costs.

_____ 6. Partially completed goods going through production.

_____ 7. The selling of products in two steps of the channel of distribution.

_____ 8. Scheduled time periods during which producers officially introduce their new lines and retail buyers shop the various lines.

_____ 9. Selling only to a limited number of stores per area to maintain exclusivity.

_____ 10. The continuous process of measuring a company's products, services, and practices against world class companies that are renowned as leaders.

_____ 11. The handling details of storing and physically moving merchandise to the proper locations.

_____ 12. Mechanically accomplished tasks done by automated equipment.

_____ 13. Buildings or complexes that house permanent showrooms of apparel manufacturers.

_____ 14. Selling only to one retailer within a certain trading area on an exclusive basis, or only to a particular chain of retail stores nationally.

_____ 15. A combination of many electronic steps of a production system, toward "hands-off" manufacturing.

_____ 16. Goods held on hand for the production process or to be sold to customers.

A. American Apparel and Footwear Association
B. *Apparel* Magazine
C. apparel marts
D. benchmarking
E. computer-integrated manufacturing (CIM)
F. confined
G. contract
H. demand flow manufacturing (DFM)
I. dual distribution
J. fiscal period
K. inventories
L. inventory control
M. logistics
N. market week
O. materials handling
P. open distribution policy
Q. robotics
R. sales forecasting
S. selected distribution policy
T. showrooms
U. technology transfer
V. total quality management (TQM)
W. trademark
X. trunk show
Y. warehouse
Z. work-in-process

(Continued)

Name_____

_____ 17. A trade name or logo that associates a product with a particular manufacturer or seller.

_____ 18. The leading business and technology trade journal for apparel industry executives and decision makers.

_____ 19. An ongoing quality process focusing on internal requirements for continuous improvement of products and customer satisfaction.

_____ 20. Computerized custom production that responds to single orders of desired goods.

_____ 21. Company-owned sales areas where merchandise is displayed and selling staffs answer questions and take orders.

_____ 22. A financial accounting period, usually one year.

_____ 23. All activities of goods not involved in actual production processes.

_____ 24. A written agreement between a buyer and seller, detailing all conditions of the sale.

_____ 25. A "holding facility" for storing backup stocks of supplies or finished goods.

_____ 26. The spread of technological knowledge, especially globally.

Group Pick and Pursue

Activity E   **Name** _____

Chapter 11   **Date** _____ **Period** _____

With a team of your classmates, choose one of the following activities. Do your initial planning on this page. Then prepare a group presentation to the class by using library and computer research tools, and visual aids.

A. Research the need for and development of CIM standards for effective supply chain technology coordination. Include information about bar code use, EDI, advance ship notices, standardized shipping container markings, demand flow manufacturing, etc.

B. Research the Standard Industrial Classification (SIC) numbering system of the U.S., which identifies all industries and their products. Describe how finished textile/apparel goods, with code numbers in the 2300s, are classified for reasons of identification and statistical evaluation.

C. Research how disagreements concerning contracts have been resolved in the soft goods chain. Look up arbitration and litigation. Find out about the Worth Street Textile Market Rules, the American Arbitration Association—General Arbitration Council of the Textile and Apparel Industries (AAA/GAC), and specifics about arbitration awards.

D. Research three apparel industry trade shows. Possible events to check include Texprocess Americas, International Apparel Federation (IAF) World Fashion Convention, Sourcing-at-MAGIC, Sewn Products Equipment & Suppliers of the Americas (SPESA), and the American Apparel Producers Network (AAPN) Annual Meeting.

Letter of activity chosen: _____

Members of the project/presentation team and areas of responsibility for each:

_____

_____

_____

_____

_____

_____

_____

_____

_____

_____

_____

_____

_____

_____

_____

The Retail Segment

Retail Segment Outline

Activity A   **Name** _____

Chapter 12   **Date** _____ **Period** _____

While referring to the textbook, outline Chapter 12 on this form, and write a section title, definition, or explanation where lines are provided.

The Retail Segment

I. Functional _____

   A. _____ — The central function of retailing that involves the activities of planning, buying, and selling apparel and accessories.

   B. _____ — _____

   _____

   C. _____ — _____

   _____

   D. Personnel — _____

   _____

   E. _____ — _____

   _____

II. Main _____

   A. Department stores — _____

   _____

   1. _____ — Smaller retail units owned and operated by a parent store and located in suburbs or other metropolitan areas.

   2. _____ — department stores — _____

   _____

   B. _____ — _____

   _____

   C. _____ — _____

   _____

(Continued)

Name_____

1. _____ — _____

   _____

2. Factory outlets — _____

   _____

3. _____ — _____

   _____

4. _____ — _____

   _____

5. Dollar Stores — _____

   _____

D. _____ — Retailers that carry _____ selections of

   _____ classifications of merchandise.

   1. _____ — _____

   2. Boutiques — _____

      _____

   3. _____ — _____

   4. Airport Retailers — _____

E. Nonstore retailers — _____

   1. _____ — _____

   2. _____ — Selling with communication devices, such as televisions and computers.

   3. _____ — _____

      _____

F. Other types of _____

   1. _____ — _____

      _____

   2. _____ — open sales pavilions, usually situated in central areas of shopping malls.

   3. _____ shops — _____

   4. _____ — _____

   5. _____ — _____

III. Store _____ — _____

IV. _____

E-Retailing RE-ality

Activity B   Name _____

Chapter 12   Date _____ Period_____

For a "reality check" about e-retailing, read the following statements aloud for class discussion, or privately with a class partner, with one of you reading the "opinion" and the other the "reality."

1. Opinion: Profits for e-retailers are as good or better than conventional retailers, and order fulfillment is easy to manage.

   Reality: Discounting plus limited economies of scale have held down profits, as well as inexperienced management and expensive customer service policies. Also, fulfillment and product return costs have been higher than expected.

2. Opinion: Brand recognition and loyalty can be built quickly and cheaply on the Internet.

   Reality: National brand-building requires huge advertising expenditures, and then may not even be effective.

3. Opinion: Developing a retail website is mainly a one-time expense.

   Reality: Creating an up-to-date retail site costs multimillions of dollars, and keeping the site competitive requires continual spending.

4. Opinion: Internet operations are virtual rather than real, thus capital expenses are less and financial returns are higher.

   Reality: Although pure e-retailers don't have to invest in stores, many must spend more on technology, inventory, and fulfillment facilities. Many pure e-retailers have failed.

5. Opinion: Most consumers are uncomfortable shopping online.

   Reality: Many people feel empowered shopping online because of the self-pace, expectations of discovery, and ability to abandon their shopping cart if they so desire.

6. Opinion: It is hard for e-retailers to target their markets, since the Internet is global.

   Reality: Besides knowing the number of "hits" a website has, e-retailers can tell who was there, what they purchased, and can send "alerts" to them about similar merchandise.

7. Opinion: Items offered on e-retailing sites are older merchandise because of the technology processes needed to include them.

   Reality: Websites get merchandise information to consumers quickly, often faster than the goods are available in stores.

8. Opinion: There is no way for retailers to get e-retailing industry information or evaluate how effective e-retailing sites are with consumers.

   Reality: Firms can subscribe to *Internet Retailer* magazine, attend the NRF Annual Convention & EXPO, or check consumer rankings on a retail shopping evaluation site.

9. Opinion: E-retailing is a revolution that is radically changing retailing as we know it.

   Reality: E-retailing is an evolution of retailing, just as malls, mail-order, and TV retailing have been. It is becoming another mainstream way to conduct day-to-day retail selling.

The Retail Life Cycle

Activity C   **Name** _____

Chapter 12   **Date** _____   **Period**_____

Complete the following exercise about the retail life cycle.

Similar to the fashion cycle (studied in Chapter 2), there is also a business life cycle for retail firms. At each stage, retailers must be willing to adapt their merchandise and store operations to consumer expectations, competitive actions, and economic conditions. This reduces business risks and takes advantage of opportunities in the market.

- Stage 1 is INNOVATION. It is based on technological, operational, and/or marketing innovations. What types of retailers (from text chart 12-7) do you think are in this stage at the present time?

  _____

  _____

- Stage 2 is GROWTH, during which there are rapid sales increases, high profits, and reinvestment in more stores. Name four types of retailers that you think are in this stage at the present time.

  _____

  _____

- Stage 3 is MATURITY, in which there is increased competition, a leveling of sales, moderate profits, operational complexity, and overstored markets. These stores try to adjust their merchandise and operations to bring in shoppers and maintain acceptable profit levels. Name four types of retailers you think are in this stage at the present time.

  _____

  _____

- Stage 4 is DECLINE. It is marked with losses in market share, marginal profitability, and an inability to compete. What types of retailers do you think are in this stage at the present time?

  _____

  _____

The trend in retailing over recent decades has revolved around the "three **v's**:"

    value: the best merchandise at the lowest price. This is accomplished with discount pricing, unique items, and efficiency/convenience of location, floor layout, and shopping.

    volume: continuously selling large amounts of merchandise.

    velocity: moving goods quickly through stores to reduce inventory and operating costs.

Analyze a specific store that is in the growth stage of the retail life cycle in relation to the three **v's**.

_____

_____

_____

Retail Functions

Activity D

Chapter 12

Name _____

Date _____ **Period** _____

Join with four other students in your class, each of you taking a different retail functional area of responsibility as summarized in text chart 12-4. As a group, choose what type of retail company you work for (either imaginary or real). Individually fill in the requested information below and give a presentation to the rest of the class with your combined knowledge.

Name of Group Member	Retail Functional Responsibility
1.	
2.	
3.	
4.	
5.	

Explain in detail the type of retailer your group works for (general or specialized merchandiser, chain department store, resort boutique, mail-order company, etc.).

_____

_____

What are the particular duties for the functional area for which you are responsible?

_____

_____

Do you work at a corporate office, flagship store, or other location? Explain.

_____

_____

How would you manage resources in the best way to satisfy customers, while helping the company make a good profit?

_____

_____

Would you hire outside experts to help you, employ a staff of experts, or do it all yourself? Why?

_____

_____

How could all of you working together for the company combine your efforts for great retail success?

_____

_____

Retail Matching

Activity E   Name _____

Chapter 12   Date _____   Period_____

Match the following terms and definitions by placing the correct letter next to each number.

_____ 1. The "parent" or original main store of a retail company that usually houses the executive, merchandising, and promotional offices for the entire operation.

_____ 2. Trade publication of the National Retail Federation.

_____ 3. Manufacturer-owned and operated discount stores that sell only the merchandise the manufacturer makes, at reduced prices.

_____ 4. Major chain and department stores that provide the attraction needed to draw customers to shopping centers or malls.

_____ 5. Another term for mail-order retailing.

_____ 6. The combining under common ownership of several chains or companies that are at the same location on the channel of distribution.

_____ 7. Selling goods through a combination of computer or mobile technologies with marketing and merchandising.

_____ 8. The world's largest retail trade association.

_____ 9. Retailers that market all types of goods in multiple price ranges, and try to satisfy many needs of a broad range of customers.

_____ 10. Independent owner-operated stores run by a husband and wife or a proprietor and a few employees.

_____ 11. Large discount specialty chains that carry huge selections of merchandise in a single product category at such low prices that they destroy the competition in their specialty area.

_____ 12. Retailers of large amounts of staple goods and mass-produced garments.

_____ 13. Theory about the evolutionary process in which stores that feature low prices gradually upgrade themselves.

_____ 14. Retailers that offer limited lines of related products targeted to more defined customers.

_____ 15. Selling to consumers by showing and describing merchandise on certain TV channels.

_____ 16. Open sales pavilions, usually situated in central areas of shopping malls.

A. anchor stores
B. category killers
C. electronic retailing
D. direct-mail marketing
E. factory outlets
F. flagship store
G. general merchandisers
H. horizontal integration
I. kiosks and carts
J. mass merchandisers
K. mom and pop stores
L. National Retail Federation
M. specialized merchandisers
N. *STORES* magazine
O. television retailing
P. wheel of retailing

Retail Positioning

Retailing Myth or Truth

Activity A Name _____

Chapter 13 Date _____ Period _____

After reading each of the following statements, indicate if you think the statement is a myth or a truth by checking the appropriate column. Then turn to the back of this page to check your answers. Later, discuss the statements as a class.

	Myth	Truth
1. Both upscale specialty stores and discount chain operations want to have a luxurious ambiance to make shoppers feel good.	_____	_____
2. Recently, retailers have been allowing their stores in neighborhood shopping centers to run-down, because the market size and profits at those locations are not worth the fix-up costs.	_____	_____
3. Store entrances should be designed for comfort, convenience, and for guiding customers safely into the store.	_____	_____
4. Category killers are also known in the industry as "big boxes."	_____	_____
5. Through market research, Talbots and other upscale specialty stores place new store locations in the middle of clusters of ZIP codes where catalog customers spend the most on their type of apparel.	_____	_____
6. The combined storage/office space of stores is usually about equal in size to the selling floor space.	_____	_____
7. For the best visibility by consumers, stores should be placed on their sites either very far back from the road or directly next to the street.	_____	_____
8. Retailers in malls must pay "common area maintenance" (CAM) charges that cover the cleaning, care, and security of the general areas of their mall.	_____	_____
9. Electronic "hybrid modeling" combines a variety of prediction techniques to estimate consumer behavior in a scientific way. This is being used to forecast sales success for proposed locations for new stores.	_____	_____
10. In the past two decades, the amount of retail space has decreased in relation to the rate of population growth.	_____	_____
11. While Walmart is dedicated to EDLP (everyday low pricing), and Sears tried and dropped EDLP, Nordstrom uses a related pricing strategy known as EDFP (everyday fair pricing).	_____	_____
12. Stores that provide entertainment value have moved to the next level of the retailing evolution. By putting entertainment in the shopping area, or locating adjacent to a large entertainment center, they give their customers reasons to stay and shop, and reasons to return.	_____	_____

(Continued)

Name _____

1. *Myth*. Upscale stores want to provide their elite customers with a luxurious ambiance to support their high prices. However, discount chains that emphasize self-service prefer a "bare bones" atmosphere as a means of promoting their low prices.

2. *Myth*. Recently, retailers have been "dressing up" the stores in neighborhood shopping centers, since the market size and profits are adequate and costs are much less to remodel those locations than to pay the higher rents at big shopping centers.

3. *Truth*. Entrances should have good lighting, flat nonskid surfaces, no clutter, and easy-to-open doors that are wide enough for people with disabilities or those who are carrying babies or packages.

4. *Truth*. Constant "big box" construction of category killer stores took place along major suburban roadways in the U.S. during the 1990s and some continues today.

5. *Truth*. This strategy is especially used by retailers who have both catalog and store businesses, and takes advantage of synergies between the two forms of retail.

6. *Myth*. Storage and office space is as small as possible because stores don't "ring up sales" from their back rooms. During store layout planning, the back area is low on the list of spatial and locational priorities.

7. *Myth*. Reduced visibility results either from setting the store too far back or too close to the street. Ideally, a store should be set back far enough to give passersby a broad perspective of the entire store, but close enough to let them read major store signs and see window displays.

8. *Truth*. The CAM charges include locking and unlocking the mall entrances, sweeping central walkways, maintaining mall restrooms, mall signs and lighting, snow plowing or repaving parking lots, etc. All stores must contribute to the costs for these services.

9. *Truth*. Computer programs can now evaluate site selections, which many companies had decided by "gut feelings" in the past. Hundreds of information variables about geographic areas and customer preferences are fed into the system, with computer results pinpointing a site in a specified market. But just to be sure, most retail companies combine that with "gut feel!"

10. *Myth*. Retail space, especially in suburban malls, has increased at a much faster rate than population growth. This has resulted in more retail space than the population needs, with stores competing for market share and having to price merchandise low to attract shoppers.

11. *Truth*. Sears dropped EDLP because its customers preferred frequent price promotions (markdown sales events), often called Hi/Lo pricing. Retailers who have had the most success with EDLP are the ones who adopted the strategy from the beginning and stayed with it, rather than having started with other approaches and turned to EDLP later. The more upscale Nordstrom uses everyday fair pricing (EDFP).

12. *Truth*. Shoppertainment, including theme restaurants and virtual reality experiences, draw traffic. When stores are combined with a variety of games, activities, rides, restaurants, play areas, and movie theaters at a convenient site, and the entertainment venues and retail assortments are "cross-promoted," consumers will come, stay, shop, and return!

Retail Advertising

Activity B   **Name** _____

Chapter 13   **Date** _____ **Period** _____

From your own knowledge and the retail advertisements, articles, and flyer inserts of a current newspaper (Sunday editions are the best), pick three distinctly different retailers to analyze and compare in this chart. After filling in the chart, attach examples of the retailers' advertising to support your answers.

	Retailer A	**Retailer B**	**Retailer C**
Name of retailer/ company			
Type of retailer (see Chapter 12)			
Describe the **target market** of retailers			
Buying motives of the retailer's customers			
Image of the retailer			
Marketing mix:			
Product			
Price			
Place			
Promotion			
Other remarks			

Retail Positioning Puzzle

Activity C   Name _____

Chapter 13   Date _____   Period _____

Define the meaning of the title of the textbook chapter, which is printed vertically for you in this chart. Then horizontally fill in the open squares of the chart to write the terms that are defined on the next page.

2.								**R**								
3.								**E**								
4.								**T**								
5.								**A**								
6.								**I**								
7.								**L**								
8.								**P**								
9.								**O**								
10.								**S**								
11.								**I**								
12.								**T**								
13.								**I**								
14.								**O**								
15.								**N**								
16.								**I**								
17.								**N**								
18.								**G**								

(Continued)

Name_____

1. Retail positioning is _____

_____

_____

2. These policies are specific guidelines, established by management, to make the store appealing for the target market through physical appearance and customer services.

3. This assortment is the number of different categories or classifications of merchandise offered by a retail store.

4. This market coverage has enough locations to adequately cover selected target markets.

5. This retail pricing strategy offers consistently fair prices and good values at all times.

6. These motives are the reasons why people buy what they buy.

7. This pricing strategy sells items below the price suggested by vendors of the goods.

8. This assortment is the quantity of each item offered in the categories or classifications carried by a retail store.

9. These motives involve consumer purchases based on qualities or images of certain products, such as materials, construction, style, fit, or guarantees.

10. This market coverage uses one retail location to serve either an entire market area or some major segment of that market.

11. This type of competition is rivalry between two or more companies using the same type of business format.

12. This type of competition is rivalry between businesses for consumers' time and money.

13. These policies, established by management, are guidelines for the company to follow to keep inventory choices on track.

14. These motives are reasons why customers choose to shop at one store rather than another, based on reputation and image, merchandise assortments, convenience of location, customer services, price, or other factors.

15. This type of competition is rivalry between two or more companies using different types of business formats to sell the same type of merchandise.

16. This type of competition is rivalry between businesses at different levels of the supply chain, such as competing with a company's own customers.

17. This market coverage serves all customers of a market by blanketing the area.

18. This pricing strategy sets high prices on items to attract customers who want quality goods or the status of owning expensive and exclusive merchandise.

Retail Positioning Tree

Activity D   Name _____

Chapter 13   Date _____   Period_____

Fill in this tree with the correct terms that fit into the blanks and are defined on the next page.

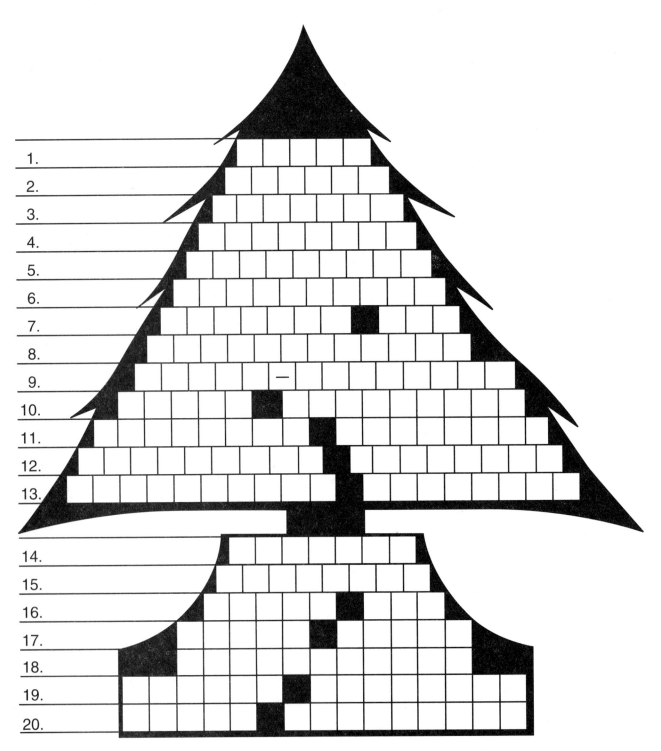

1.
2.
3.
4.
5.
6.
7.
8.
9.
10.
11.
12.
13.
14.
15.
16.
17.
18.
19.
20.

(Continued)

Name _____

1. An _____ is how something or someone is perceived by others, or nonverbal communication of a retailer in customers' minds.

2. The _____ mix of a shopping center or mall is the particular assortment of different types of stores grouped together there.

3. _____ business districts are downtown retailing clusters.

4. _____ shopping centers group many stores together, often in an enclosed mall with several shopping levels and one or more full-line anchors.

5. _____ shopping centers are medium-sized clusters of 15 to 50 stores that serve community markets within a five- to six-mile radius.

6. An _____ is the diversification of goods, range of stock, or total selection offered by a retailer.

7. A company's _____ is its entire selection of goods and services.

8. _____ shopping centers are small clusters, with five to 15 stores, that service local consumers in surrounding neighborhoods.

9. _____ centers are the largest malls and shopping areas, also called "power centers" or "mega malls."

10. _____ is advertising special price reductions of goods to bring in shoppers who will then buy other items as well.

11. _____ is a response of conscious reasoning.

12. _____ is a response based on feeling.

13. _____ is the way consumers act in the market.

14. The total of all the signs of a store or location is _____.

15. _____ is atmosphere.

16. A _____ is when competitors drastically lower their prices to try to attract customers by underselling each other.

17. _____ are unenclosed (open) shopping areas that have a line of stores along an outside walkway.

18. _____ is when consumers see and evaluate merchandise in stores and then comparison shop digitally to buy at the lowest price online.

19. _____ is the amount of concentration a retailer has in a customer area, such as intensive, selective, or exclusive.

20. _____ is the retail function that involves advertising, display, public relations, publicity, and special events to encourage public acceptance and sales of products.

Retail Positioning Facts

Activity E   **Name** _____

Chapter 13   **Date** _____ **Period**_____

As you review the chapter, answer the following questions.

1. What usually happens when retailers try to offer something for everyone? _____
   _____

2. List at least three ways that managers can stay in touch with their customers. _____
   _____
   _____
   _____

3. Retail merchandising and operational policies are monitored carefully in relation to what three
   major factors? _____
   _____
   _____
   _____

4. Do fashion purchases usually involve higher amounts of rational buying motives or emotional
   ones? How do fashion marketers appeal to that? _____
   _____
   _____
   _____

5. Are product and patronage motives based on rational or emotional buying motives? _____
   _____
   _____
   _____

6. What type of competition do restaurants have with retail stores? _____
   _____

7. Name at least six services that might be offered by upscale, or higher price, quality stores.
   _____
   _____
   _____
   _____
   _____
   _____

(Continued)

Name _____

8. Briefly describe the ambiance of upscale stores, mid-priced stores, and low-priced discount stores.

_____

_____

_____

9. To present the proper store image, what attitudes and appearance should employees have?

_____

_____

10. What would happen if a store attracts shoppers at a certain fashion level because of its advertising, but stocks merchandise different than projected? _____

_____

_____

11. How might a store go about changing its image, to add new customers while keeping its old customers? _____

_____

_____

12. Describe a broad and shallow merchandise assortment, and the type of store that would stock it.

_____

_____

13. What types of stores stock assortments of moderate breadth and depth? _____

_____

_____

14. What is the "right price" for certain goods? _____

_____

_____

15. How does price level enable overall profits to be similar between some retailers that sell low volumes and others that sell high volumes of goods? _____

_____

_____

16. What is a price line selling policy? _____

_____

17. To what two general areas does place strategy relate? _____

_____

_____

(Continued)

Name _____

18. What groups of consumers shop in central business districts? _____

_____

_____

19. Describe lifestyle centers. _____

_____

_____

20. Why can prestigious specialty retailers use the exclusive market coverage approach? _____

_____

_____

21. What are the three main considerations when evaluating a store's position on its site? _____

_____

_____

_____

22. What is the main consumer criticism of mall shopping? _____

_____

_____

23. Lately, what three types of retailers have increased in popularity?

_____

_____

_____

24. In shopping malls that feature entertainment, how do shopping and entertainment compete and not compete? _____

_____

_____

_____

_____

Retail Merchandise

Apparel Merchandise Categories

Activity A   Name _____

Chapter 14   Date _____ Period_____

From catalogs, newspaper/magazine advertisements, or retail websites, find four pictures of apparel garments (not accessories)—one each for women, men, infants, and children. Mount them in the boxes and respond to the questions and statements.

Womenswear category:

Into what merchandise classification does the garment fall?

_____

In what sizes is the item offered? _____

_____

Describe the merchandise item, by brand, style, etc. _____

_____

Describe something interesting that you notice about this particular item. _____

_____

_____

Menswear category:

Into what merchandise classification does the garment fall?

_____

In what sizes is the item offered? _____

_____

Describe the merchandise item, by brand, style, etc. _____

_____

Describe something interesting that you notice about this particular item. _____

_____

_____

(Continued)

Name _____

Infantswear category:

Although no merchandise classifications were shown in the text chapter, name one into which you believe the garment would fit. _____

_____

In what sizes is the item offered? _____

_____

Describe the merchandise item, by brand, style, etc. _____

_____

Describe something interesting that you notice about this particular item (comfort, practicality, etc.). _____

_____

_____

Childrenswear category:

Although no merchandise classifications were shown in the text chapter, name one into which you believe the garment would fit. _____

_____

In what sizes is the item offered? _____

_____

Describe the merchandise item, by brand, style, etc. _____

_____

_____

Describe something interesting that you notice about this particular item (growth features, self-help features, etc.).

_____

_____

Accessories

Activity B	**Name** _____
Chapter 14	**Date** _____ **Period** _____

Complete the following exercise about accessories.

1. What are accessories?

   _____

   _____

2. How can accessories extend and add variety to wardrobes?

   _____

   _____

3. Name at least three classic pieces of jewelry that tend to remain in style.

   _____

   _____

   _____

4. Find pictures from catalogs or magazines of outfits that include three different categories of accessories. Mount them here. Discuss, as if you are a retail salesperson talking to a customer, how each accessory enhances the garment(s) with which it is worn. Also mention other ways the garment(s) might be accessorized.

   A. _____

   _____

   _____

   _____

   _____

   _____

   _____

   _____

   _____

   _____

   _____

   _____

   _____

   _____

(Continued)

Name _____

B. _____

C. _____

Retail Terms Differences

Activity C   **Name** _____

Chapter 14   **Date** _____ **Period**_____

Complete the following exercise to distinguish between retailing terms.

In relation to this chapter, what is the difference between:

1. Hardlines and softlines? _____

   _____

   _____

   _____

2. Women's and petite's apparel size categories? _____

   _____

   _____

   _____

3. Double-ticket and half-sizes? _____

   _____

   _____

   _____

4. Active sportswear and suit separates? _____

   _____

   _____

   _____

5. Infants and toddlers? _____

   _____

   _____

   _____

6. Self-help features and growth features? _____

   _____

   _____

   _____

7. Impulse purchases and substitutable goods? _____

   _____

   _____

   _____

(Continued)

Name _____

8. Fine jewelry and bridge jewelry? _____

_____

_____

_____

9. Extenders and costume jewelry? _____

_____

_____

_____

10. Cosmetics and toiletries? _____

_____

_____

_____

11. Fragrances and brand-line representatives? _____

_____

_____

_____

12. Downsize and dual sizing? _____

_____

_____

_____

13. Footwear and hosiery? _____

_____

_____

_____

14. Prestige cosmetic lines and mass market cosmetic lines? _____

_____

_____

_____

Retail Merchandise Questions

Activity D   Name _____

Chapter 14   Date _____ Period_____

Write thought-provoking multiple choice questions with information contained in the following main chapter sections. Write the letter of each correct answer on another piece of paper and exchange questions with a classmate to try to answer each other's questions correctly.

Women's Apparel (Women's apparel sizes and women's apparel classifications):

1. _____

    a. _____

    b. _____

    c. _____

    d. _____

2. _____

    a. _____

    b. _____

    c. _____

    d. _____

Men's Apparel (Production of menswear lines, men's apparel sizes and classifications):

3. _____

    a. _____

    b. _____

    c. _____

    d. _____

4. _____

    a. _____

    b. _____

    c. _____

    d. _____

(Continued)

Name_____

Infants' and Children's Apparel (Attitudes, sizes/features, toddlers, children, older children, etc.):

5. _____

   a. _____

   b. _____

   c. _____

   d. _____

6. _____

   a. _____

   b. _____

   c. _____

   d. _____

Accessories (all categories):

7. _____

   a. _____

   b. _____

   c. _____

   d. _____

8. _____

   a. _____

   b. _____

   c. _____

   d. _____

Cosmetics Industry Products:

9. _____

   a. _____

   b. _____

   c. _____

   d. _____

Planning to Buy

Planning Sales and Stock Turnover

Activity A

Chapter 15

Name _____

Date _____ Period_____

Read the following explanation. Then complete the problems on the following page.

Retail profits are largely determined by maintaining a proper relationship of inventories, prices, and sales.

A **dollar merchandise plan** schedules sales month-by-month for a 6-month (seasonal) period, the amount of stock planned for each of these months, and an estimate of markup and markdown percentages. A dollar sales goal (**seasonal planned sales**) is forecast first. Then the inventory needed to meet the goal is planned; to be purchased for the proper timing and in the correct amounts.

Seasonal planned sales = last year's sales +/− [last year's sales × planned increase/decrease %]

For instance, if last year's same-season sales were $400,000, and a 5% sales increase is expected this year (possibly because of new fashion trends and an aggressive promotional program):

Seasonal planned sales = $400,000 + [$400,000 × 5% sales increase projection] =
$400,000 + [$400,000 × .05] = $400,000 + $20,000 = $**420,000**

Two specific seasonal planned sales figures can be added together for an **annual planned sales** estimate, or one seasonal planned sales figure can be multiplied by 2 for a less precise estimate:

$420,000 seasonal planned sales × 2 = approximate annual planned sales

Also, the annual planned sales estimate can be divided into different sized monthly sales projections according to usual sales volumes in those months (based on past years' sales records).

After **planned monthly sales** are established, the amount of dollar stock needed at the beginning of each month (BOM stocks) and/or end of each month (EOM stocks) must be determined. Each month's BOM stocks figure is the same as the previous month's EOM stocks. For instance, April BOM stocks of $70,000 are also the $70,000 amount of EOM stocks for March.

Stock turnover represents the balance between sales and inventory. It is the number of times that an average stock is sold (turned into money) and replaced during a given period. The time period is usually one year, but can be computed on a weekly, monthly, or seasonal basis. See text illustration 15-9. Retailers who are able to raise their stock turnover rate are more efficient merchandisers. They make better use of capital, control inventories better, and gain higher profits.

(Continued)

Name_____

$$\text{Stock turnover} = \frac{\$ \text{ retail sales for period}}{\$ \text{ average stock for same period (see next equation)}}$$

$$\text{Average stock} = \frac{\$ \text{ total of all months' beginning inventories + ending inventory for the period}}{\text{The number of inventories}}$$

For instance, if retail sales for a 6-month period were $800,000, and the average stock was $200,000 (total of inventories/7), turnover for the period would be $800,000/$200,000 = **4**.

Problems (Show your procedure whenever possible. A calculator may be used.)

1. For the spring season last year, sales of the women's better dresses department were $450,000. A 5% increase in sales is expected for this spring season because of pent-up demand. What is the dollar value of seasonal planned sales? _____

2. For the fall season last year, sales of the men's suit department were $300,000. A 2% decrease in sales is expected for this fall season (because of poor economic conditions and competition from a new store nearby). What is the dollar value of seasonal planned sales? _____

3. On the basis of the following chart, what are total sales for the period? _____

Date	Retail Inventory (stock on hand)	Sales
August 1	$38,000	$20,000
September 1	$46,000	$26,000
October 1	$52,000	$28,000
November 1	$55,000	$30,000
December 1	$45,000	$24,000
January 1	$22,000	$12,000
January 31	$22,000	

4. How did you calculate the total sales for the period? _____

_____

5. Without having specific sales numbers for the other six months of the year, what might the annual planned sales estimate be? _____

6. What is the EOM stock figure for December 31? _____

7. What is the average stock for the period shown in the chart above? _____

8. Determine the seasonal stock turnover on the basis of the information in #3-7 above.

_____

9. If seasonal stock turnover is for a 6-month period, what might the annual stock turnover be?

_____

Working with Stock-to-Sales Ratio and OTB

Activity B

Chapter 15

Name _____

Date _____ Period_____

Read the following explanation. Then complete the problems on the following page.

Monthly inventory figures needed for the beginning of each month (or other period) are usually planned with a **stock-to-sales ratio**. Since a wide selection of merchandise is needed for customers to make choices, the ratio is used to balance planned monthly stocks with planned monthly sales. The ratio indicates how many items are needed, per item that sells. Generally, a ratio is already determined that has provided good sales performance in the past (or one that is an industry norm for that product line). Also, since consumer choices vary according to seasons and holidays, different ratios might be established for individual months. Retail buyers decide how much inventory is needed at the beginning of individual months (BOM—See Activity A.) by:

BOM stock needed = planned monthly sales × stock-to-sales ratio

For instance, the sportswear department has planned sales of $50,000 for the month of July. Past experience for the department's sales in July show that a 3.7 stock-to-sales ratio has been the most successful (3.7 items are needed to each item that sells). Thus, stock at the beginning of the month should be:

BOM July stock needed = $50,000 × 3.7 = **$185,000**

Open-to-buy (OTB) is a control figure that represents the dollar amount of merchandise the buyer may receive during the balance of a given period (usually one month), without exceeding the planned stock figure at the end of that period. It is the amount of unspent buying money for purchases to be received during the period. It is the difference between the planned purchases for a period and the merchandise orders already placed or received for that period.

OTB for the balance of the month = planned purchases for the month

– merchandise already received for the month

– outstanding orders to be delivered during the month

For instance, a certain buyer has planned April purchases of $60,000. The store's records indicate that from April 1 to April 15 the department received $35,000 worth of new goods and there are orders of $12,000 more goods to be delivered during April. The OTB balance for the month is:

OTB for the balance of the month =

$60,000 planned April purchases

– 35,000 goods already received

– 12,000 goods on order
_____

$13,000 April OTB balance

OTB identifies the difference between actual results and planned goals so the buyer can take corrective measures when needed. The planned purchase figure for a particular month indicates the sum available to purchase goods during the month, but does not indicate the distribution of the money throughout the month. Buyers usually distribute purchases over the entire month to reorder or replace fast-selling goods, fill in stocks so complete stocks are offered, take advantage of special purchase opportunities, or test new items or resources.

(Continued)

Name_____

Problems (Show your procedure whenever possible. A calculator may be used.)

1. Holiday sales are always heavy and are very important to the profit of the sweater department. Ample stock must be on hand. Determine the BOM stock figure for December (inventory on hand on 12/1) for the department, with planned sales of $180,000 and a planned stock-to-sales ratio for the month of 6.3.

2. Each January, after the holiday rush, the same sweater department of #1 (above) tries to sell as many as possible of the remaining items in stock. Prices are reduced to offer wonderful bargains to shoppers, resulting in sales of most of the leftover holiday goods. The department's January stock-to-sales ratio is 2.1. Why do you think the stock-to-sales ratio is so much lower for January than it is for December?

3. A new retail buyer has been told that the stock-to-sales ratio for the hosiery department during all months in the fall is 4.1. Stock at the end of October is planned to be at $147,600. Planned sales for that department in November have been calculated at $36,000. What is the BOM stock figure for November?

4. A buyer for a chain store has planned June purchases of $1,680,000 for his category of goods, to be distributed among the store's branches. $940,000 of that category of items have already been received in June and sent to the branches. Another $690,000 of goods have been ordered for June delivery, from various vendors. What is that buyer's June OTB balance?

5. What is the available OTB for a department that has planned purchases of $54,600 for February and outstanding orders of $57,200 for the month?

6. Ms. Foss, the owner of the Fashion Dress Shop, watches her open-to-buy very carefully each month. She uses one OTB figure for her small shop that includes all of her dresses, suits, scarves, jewelry, and other inventory. For September, she has planned to purchase $52,000 of stock. By September 5th, she had received $8,000 worth of dresses, $10,000 of suits, $900 of scarves, $1,100 of jewelry, and $400 of all other items. A $12,000 shipment of dresses and suits arrived early on September 16th—just in the knick of time, since dresses were almost selling faster than she could keep them in stock. How much available OTB does Ms. Foss have left for September, and for what might she use it?

Merchandise Planning Review

Activity C   **Name** _____

Chapter 15   **Date** _____ **Period**_____

As you review the first half of the book chapter, answer the following questions.

1. Briefly summarize what merchandise planning involves. _____

_____

_____

2. What group makes the final decisions about what will or will not sell through retailers? _____

_____

_____

3. A buyer for what size store would have the widest scope of job responsibilities? _____

_____

_____

4. Why do buyers need to anticipate customer demand and fashion trends many months before the
   selling season? _____

_____

_____

5. How can salespeople be a valuable source of product and customer information? _____

_____

_____

6. How can consumer opinions and behavior be formally collected? _____

_____

_____

7. What might be wrong with market information provided by vendors? _____

_____

_____

8. How do trade publications provide planning information for buyers? _____

_____

_____

9. What do the results of comparison shopping determine? _____

_____

_____

(Continued)

Name _____

10. What might result if a buyer orders less merchandise than needed? _____

_____

_____

_____

11. What is the result of proper retail planning for sufficient fashion stock to make most sales, but with a controlled dollar investment in inventory? _____

_____

_____

12. What months make up the two main planning/buying periods of the year? _____

_____

_____

13. On what is the dollar merchandise plan mainly based? _____

_____

_____

14. What is the purpose of open-to-buy? _____

_____

_____

15. Why does the stocking of more substitute products not significantly increase retail sales? _____

_____

_____

16. What is memorandum buying? _____

_____

_____

17. Define irregulars. _____

_____

_____

18. In general, why are stub-ticket control and card-control systems not satisfactory for seasonal and fashion merchandise? _____

_____

_____

Sourcing Merchandise Outline

Activity D   **Name** _____

Chapter 15   **Date** _____ **Period** _____

I. While referring to the textbook, outline the "Selecting Merchandise Resources" section near the end of Chapter 15. Write a subsection title, definition, or concise explanation where lines are provided below. Then use your outline information to do Part II at the end of the next page.

Selecting Merchandise Resources

A. Types of merchandise resources

    1. _____

    _____

    _____

    _____

    _____

    2. These middlepeople have large quantities of goods and can deliver small orders quickly to retailers. However, the prices are higher. _____

    _____

    3. _____

    _____

    _____

    _____

    _____

    4. _____

    _____

    _____

    _____

    _____

B. Evaluating vendor attributes

    1. _____

    _____

    _____

    _____

    _____

(Continued)

Name _____

2. These include payment/credit requirements, if items can be reordered, retail pricing rules, distribution practices, minimum purchase requirements, rules about accepting returns or selling clearance merchandise, confinement of goods, etc. _____

_____

3. _____

_____

_____

_____

_____

4. _____

_____

_____

_____

_____

C. Selecting specific resources _____

_____

_____

_____

_____

D. Brand names versus private label merchandise _____

_____

_____

_____

_____

E. Offshore sourcing _____

_____

_____

_____

_____

II. In a group with several other students, compare the responses on your outlines. Thoroughly discuss how important the planning process is for retailers to make good selections of merchandise resources. Also discuss the damaging results that could occur to their businesses if they are not careful in choosing their vendors.

Planning to Buy Fill-in-the-Blanks

Activity E   Name _____

Chapter 15   Date _____   Period_____

Complete the following statements by filling in the blanks.

1. Merchandise _____ involves estimating, as correctly as possible, consumer demand and how it can best be satisfied.

2. Merchandise _____ is done through vendors, such as apparel producers, to obtain the merchandise decided upon during the planning phase.

3. _____ selling is nonpersonal promotion aimed at a large general audience.

4. _____ selling is the exchange of merchandise to individual consumers in return for money or credit.

5. Merchandise planning, buying, and selling make up a _____ _____ of ongoing activity.

6. _____ _____ are merchandising professionals who are responsible for selecting and purchasing goods for their companies.

7. _____ buying is when buyers who work for department store organizations might purchase merchandise for only their own departments.

8. _____ buying is when chain store buyers typically buy only one category classification, such as men's sweaters or women's better dresses.

9. _____ books or slips are forms salespeople can use to record customer inquiries or requests about products not carried by the store or that are out of stock.

10. _____ shoppers are hired to check and report back to their employers the depth of merchandise assortments, prices, ambiance, and services offered in competing and noncompeting stores.

11. _____ _____, or inventory turns, is the number of times the inventory is sold and replaced in a given period, or how fast merchandise goes in and out of the store.

12. Buyers prepare _____ _____ that describe the type and quantities of merchandise to purchase for their departments or stores for a specific time period and for a set amount of money.

13. A _____ _____ _____ is an estimated dollar amount, or budget, for planned stock, sales, and profit for the department for a six-month period.

14. Based on past sales figures of how fast particular items of a department or category sell, the _____-_____-_____ _____ is calculated to determine stock needed at the beginning of each month.

15. _____-_____-_____ is the dollar or merchandise unit amount that buyers are permitted to order for their stores, departments, or apparel classifications for a specified time period.

16. An _____ _____ projects the variety and quantity of specific stockkeeping units to be carried by a store or department to meet customer demand.

17. A _____-_____ _____ is the smallest unit for which sales and stock records are kept.

18. A _____ _____ _____ is a proposed purchase list composed mostly of commodity goods, such as blue jeans, underwear, hosiery, and men's dress shirts.

(Continued)

Name_____

19. A _____ _____ _____ is composed mostly of fashion merchandise and includes items that have strong customer appeal for a limited time.

20. A _____-_____ list contains key items or best-selling items that should always be on hand and on display.

21. _____ _____ are items purchased to supplement or accessorize other products.

22. _____ _____ is when a retailer submits definite specifications to a manufacturer rather than looking for goods already produced.

23. In _____ buying, the retailer displays and sells goods owned by the supplier and deducts an agreed-upon commission.

24. _____ _____-_____ buying involves the writing of purchase orders for merchandise from vendors at regular price during market times, as well as later reorders.

25. _____ buying is ordering merchandise well ahead of the desired shipment date, usually at a lower price.

26. _____ buying is the purchase of items at special low prices to be offered at reduced prices to the store's customers. It is sometimes called clearance merchandise.

27. With _____-_____ _____, the salesperson removes a specific portion of the price ticket when the item is sold.

28. The _____-_____ system has a separate card for each item stocked so that at the end of the day, information from sales slips are tallied, posted to the cards, and deducted from the listed inventory.

29. To oversee stock conditions, most retailers now use fast and accurate computerized _____-_____ systems that include electronic scanners.

30. Today's stock control technology, called _____ _____-_____-_____ equipment, offers improved inventory cost reduction without sacrificing customer goodwill.

31. With _____-_____ _____, retail buyers and their suppliers establish specific stock level and replenishment criteria so EPOS data that goes to the suppliers' computers calculates what and how much new inventory is needed from each store.

32. To maximize vendor services, the concept of _____-_____ _____, shipped to the store in a condition to be put directly onto the selling floor without any additional preparation by retail employees, is gaining in use.

33. _____ time is how soon the vendor can deliver goods after they have been ordered.

34. _____ _____ is the term used when goods are bought from overseas producers or when private label goods are contracted with foreign manufacturing plants.

35. An _____ _____ is the price at which one country's money can be converted into another's.

Merchandise Buying

The When and Where of Merchandise Buying

Activity A   **Name** _____

Chapter 16   **Date** _____ **Period**_____

As you review the first half of the book chapter, respond to the following questions and statements.

1. How far ahead of the selling season do buyers place their main orders for merchandise? _____

   _____

2. When is planning for promotion and advertising to consumers about the new merchandise started? _____

   _____

   _____

   _____

3. What is the most common method of doing major buying, as well as making contacts with new sources? _____

   _____

   _____

4. Why might a vendor provide refreshments for buyers during a market week? _____

   _____

   _____

   _____

5. Name at least three ways that producers might show their lines during market weeks. _____

   _____

   _____

   _____

6. Besides learning about fashion trends (colors, styles, and fabrications), what market condition factors might be gained by buyers during market weeks? _____

   _____

   _____

   _____

(Continued)

Name_____

7. Why might buyers get special terms and purchases during market weeks? _____

_____

_____

8. How can networking with other buyers during market weeks help a retail buyer? _____

_____

_____

9. What are the two main locations where ideas for new merchandise display techniques are found?

_____

_____

10. To what size retailers do apparel trade shows cater? _____

_____

11. Name at least four cities with major apparel marts. _____

_____

_____

_____

12. When, during mart market weeks, do combined fashion shows take place? _____

_____

_____

13. What do buyers receive at introductory mart orientation programs? _____

_____

_____

14. For what types of apparel is the Miami market known? _____

_____

_____

15. What market location is the fashion center for the Pacific Northwestern states? _____

_____

16. A rule that guides retail buyers is: "Whatever is purchased must be able to sell." Purchasing the
    right future merchandise for the store's customers is more than half the job of sales. React to this
    in the space provided. _____

_____

_____

_____

A Buying Team

Activity B	**Name** _____	
Chapter 16	**Date** _____	**Period** _____

Form a retail "buying team" with a group of classmates. Pretend to be buyers for a particular type of apparel retailer. After considering the following questions, explain your buying trip in detail to the rest of the class. Tell why you made each decision.

Type of retailer and target market:

_____

Description of the retailer's location or selling venue:

_____

_____

The fashion season for which you are about to buy:

_____

Buying location and length of visit:

_____

Will this be the only buying trip for the season or one of several?

_____

The types of financial, merchandising, and other details that should be planned before going:

_____

_____

The type(s) of buying resources to be used (consider cost issues as well as advantages of using service providers):

_____

_____

Estimate of costs for travel, lodging, meals, etc. (check websites for prices of planes, trains, hotels, etc.):

_____

_____

Should any details be reevaluated because of cost (length of stay, distance to market, etc.)?

_____

(Continued)

Name_____

Itinerary of what you think your time schedule will be like while at market (to make the best use of your time):

_____

_____

_____

_____

_____

_____

_____

_____

_____

_____

_____

_____

_____

_____

_____

_____

_____

_____

_____

_____

_____

_____

_____

_____

_____

_____

_____

_____

_____

_____

_____

_____

_____

Buying Term Matching

Activity C   Name _____

Chapter 16   Date _____ Period_____

Match the following terms and definitions by placing the correct letter next to each number.

_____ 1. Independent foreign buying agents who help retailers buy goods from their countries.

_____ 2. Buying at the wholesale level for resale at the retail level.

_____ 3. Scheduled time periods during which producers officially introduce their new lines and retail buyers shop the various lines.

_____ 4. Merchandise orders with a longer lead time before the delivery date.

_____ 5. Additional orders of the same goods as ordered previously.

_____ 6. Promises to buy from favored vendors over a period of time, with no detail of colors, sizes, or shipment until later.

_____ 7. The wholesale price for goods in a foreign country of origin, exclusive of shipping costs and duties.

_____ 8. The conditions governing a sale, as set forth by the seller.

_____ 9. Trusted brand or private label suppliers of specific categories of goods to retailers, selected to make decisions about merchandise for the retailers.

_____ 10. The date designated by the retailer on the PO specifying by when the goods are needed and should be delivered.

_____ 11. A detailed list of goods shipped or services rendered by the supplier, showing the money amount due from the receiving company.

_____ 12. Concentrated areas where goods are created, produced, sold, and bought at wholesale prices.

_____ 13. An arrangement in which merchandise is shipped to the retailer's store for inspections before the final purchase decision is made.

_____ 14. Retail buying term for writing completed orders with vendors, usually during market week.

_____ 15. Stock orders for line merchandise.

_____ 16. Orders placed with a resident buyer or vendor, without any restrictions as to style, color, price, or delivery.

_____ 17. A written document authorizing the delivery of certain goods at specific prices and times.

A. advance orders
B. approval buying
C. back orders
D. blanket orders
E. category captains
F. commissionaires
G. completion date
H. first cost
I. invoice
J. leave paper
K. market centers
L. market weeks
M. open orders
N. procurement
O. purchase order (PO)
P. regular orders
Q. reorders
R. resident buying offices (RBOs)
S. special orders
T. terms of sale

(Continued)

Name_____

_____ 18. Service organizations in major market centers that report market information, act as market representatives, and perform other related services to groups of noncompeting retailers.

_____ 19. Orders for merchandise to satisfy individual customers, rather than for regular stock.

_____ 20. Merchandise orders that have not been filled within the time specified, and have not been canceled by the buyer.

Purchase Order Considerations

Activity D   Name _____

Chapter 16   Date _____ Period_____

Study the information on this page and review the types of orders described in the text chapter. Then, in the same "buying team" of classmates as for Activity C, decide what imaginary merchandise should be ordered from one of the vendors visited during your pretend buying trip. Make decisions about negotiations concerning terms of sale, considering that a long-term relationship with the vendor is desired. Fill in the purchase order on the back of this page.

Most companies adjust their basic price to reward customers for early payment of bills, volume purchases, buying off season, taking odd lots, etc. Specifics about these price adjustments are often defined on the backs of printed purchase order forms.

Dating is the time period during which discounts may be taken by the retailer, and the date on which the invoice will become due for payment. Regular dating may include a cash discount agreement, with the understanding that the discount and credit periods are counted from the date of the invoice. The invoice date is usually the date the goods are shipped from the supplier. Extra dating is an agreement that allows the purchaser a specified number of days before the dating of the bill begins.

EOM dating of invoices agrees that cash discount and net credit periods begin at the end of the month. Invoices dated on the 25th of the month or later are generally treated as if dated on the first day of the next month. ROG dating of invoices specifies that the discount period allowed by the vendor does not begin until the goods are actually received by the retailer (receipt of goods).

A cash discount is a reduction in the purchase price allowed by a vendor for payment before the due date of the bill. It is usually expressed as a percentage of the billed price. For instance, a cash discount of "5/10 net 30" indicates a 5% reduction for payment within the first 10 days from the date of the invoice, with a total of 30 days before the bill (at full face value) is overdue.

A quantity discount is a price reduction offered by the seller for purchases of large volumes of goods. By law, these discounts must be offered to all customers equally, and must not exceed the seller's cost savings (for selling, inventory, transportation, etc.) associated with selling large quantities. They provide an incentive for customers to make larger purchases from fewer vendors.

A trade discount (also called a functional discount) is a reduction in price, written as "less x%," offered to wholesalers, middlepeople, and retailers by manufacturers as compensation for performing certain functions, such as storing, selling, recordkeeping, or advertising.

A seasonal discount is a price reduction to buyers who buy goods out of season. Seasonal discounts encourage early ordering and allow sellers to keep production steady during the year, such as for swimsuits in the fall and ski jackets in the spring.

FOB (free on board) point indicates that the buyer pays the shipping freight charges from the point of origin. Title to the goods passes to the buyer at the FOB point.

(Continued)

Name _____

Name of Retailer

Purchase Order # _____
Manufacturing # _____
Manufacturer _____
Address _____
City _____
Phone # _____   Fax # _____

Department #/Name _____
Date _____
Terms _____ EOM
_____ Automatically cancelled if not shipped by _____
_____ Send separate invoice and packing slip for each store
_____ Ship this entire order in one package

Style #	Class	Description	Central Store		Branch Store 1		Branch Store 2		Qty. Total	Unit Cost	Total Cost	Unit $ Retail	Total $ Retail
			Color	Sizes	Color	Sizes	Color	Sizes					
		Totals											

Shipping Instructions
Show Order # and Dept. # on all packages. Combine packages into one shipment unless otherwise instructed. Ship Roadway Express where available, or other motor truck. Insure . . .(etc.)

Billing Instructions
Mail all invoices to Accounts Payable Department, *Name and address of retailer.* Indicate Order # and Dept. # on each invoice. Invoices must be rendered by style, color, sizes. (Etc.) . . .

In accepting this order, vendor agrees to furnish a guarantee rendered in good faith that the textile fiber products specified therein are labeled in accordance with the Federal Textile Fiber Products Identification Act.

Routing exception on this order:
Via:

No order valid unless in writing on our form & countersigned.
Buyer _____
Approved _____

This order is subject to the conditions and instructions stated on this and the reverse side which are made a part thereof.

Communicating Information

Getting the Message

Activity A Name _____

Chapter 17 Date _____ Period _____

Answer the first two questions. Then think about how well you send and receive messages with family members, friends, classmates, teachers, coworkers, etc. Respond to the statements by placing check marks where appropriate. (Desirable and undesirable statements are intermingled, and there are no right or wrong answers.) Then analyze your responses at the end of the activity.

How is communication defined in business situations? _____

_____

_____

Who are the two major parties in the communication process? _____

_____

_____

	Never	Sometimes	Often
1. I read important written material with a purpose.	____	____	____
2. I look up the meaning of words that I don't know.	____	____	____
3. I look directly at someone who is speaking to me.	____	____	____
4. I interrupt others while they are talking.	____	____	____
5. I pay attention and stay focused when someone is talking.	____	____	____
6. I ask questions if I don't understand what has been said.	____	____	____
7. I have a hard time concentrating on what someone is saying to me when there is background "noise."	____	____	____
8. Others don't seem to listen to me when I talk.	____	____	____
9. I have to repeat what I say to others.	____	____	____
10. I seem to dominate most conversations.	____	____	____
11. My thoughts are well organized when I speak to others.	____	____	____
12. I bore people with unnecessary details when I talk, or act like an expert on the subject when I'm not.	____	____	____

(Continued)

Name_____

	Never	Sometimes	Often
13. My tone of voice seems to repel those with whom I speak.	_____	_____	_____
14. I am nervous and shy when I talk to people.	_____	_____	_____
15. I look directly at the person with whom I am speaking.	_____	_____	_____
16. I talk with people rather than to them.	_____	_____	_____
17. My mind wanders during conversations.	_____	_____	_____
18. I speak slowly and clearly enough for people to understand what I am saying.	_____	_____	_____
19. I am aware of feedback and adjust my talking accordingly.	_____	_____	_____
20. My written communications are clear and concise.	_____	_____	_____
21. I use the proper form when writing letters or reports.	_____	_____	_____
22. I am cheerful and attentive during telephone conversations.	_____	_____	_____
23. I take telephone messages accurately and politely.	_____	_____	_____
24. I return phone calls as soon as possible.	_____	_____	_____
25. I am comfortable and efficient when doing tasks at the computer.	_____	_____	_____

Based upon my answers to the statements:

I would describe my reading skills as _____

_____

I would describe my listening skills as _____

_____

I would describe my speaking skills as _____

_____

I would describe my writing skills as _____

_____

I would describe my telephone skills as _____

_____

I would describe my computer skills as _____

_____

(Continued)

Name_____

The major concerns I have about my communication skills are _____

_____

_____

_____

_____

_____

_____

To become a more effective communicator I might try to _____

_____

_____

_____

_____

_____

_____

Group Communication

Activity B   **Name** _____

Chapter 17   **Date** _____ **Period** _____

With a small group of classmates, pick one of the following activities listed here. Complete the written activity, and then present your material to the rest of the class.

A. Write five sentences that might have a different encoding/decoding meaning for people who do not have a common frame of reference. The classroom students are to try to describe the two different messages that might be transmitted.

B. Write five closed-ended questions and read them out loud to the rest of the class one at a time. Ask other students to change them to open-ended questions.

C. Describe five different types of business statistics scenarios. Have other students say what type of graph, chart, etc., would be the best visual aid to convey the data and explain why.

1. _____

_____

_____

_____

2. _____

_____

_____

_____

3. _____

_____

_____

_____

4. _____

_____

_____

_____

5. _____

_____

_____

_____

Added Communications

Activity C   Name _____

Chapter 17   Date _____ Period_____

Read the following statements and place a check if you think the statement is an interesting aspect of fashion business communication, or if it seems uninteresting to you. You will not be graded on your responses. Then choose what you feel the most interesting statement of the group is and explain your reaction to it in detail.

Interesting   Uninteresting

_____   _____   1. Statistics can be impressively presented in different ways. Data is sometimes manipulated to make a situation appear to be something it isn't. It is important to change statistics into meaningful, usable information.

_____   _____   2. It has been said that only 7% of communication is words. Almost all the rest is body language and tone of voice. Thus, voice mail and e-mail can be misunderstood if not carefully phrased.

_____   _____   3. Communication effectiveness is one of businesses' greatest challenges. The "information loop" is the group of people through which a piece of information is spread. The loop should include everyone who needs to know, but should not include others to whom the information would only muddle their brains with data overload!

_____   _____   4. Types of business letters include: those that request information, merchandise, or service; those that give good news or a neutral message; and those that deliver bad news. The tone and wording of each is very different and important.

_____   _____   5. Senders and receivers must have a common frame of reference to communicate. One retail shop owner might say to another, "Back to school was real soft—good traffic, but no bags." The other retail shop owner would know that means, "The late summer back-to-school selling season was not very profitable. There were lots of shoppers, but very few purchases."

_____   _____   6. Line graphs are good for showing business trends. Bar charts compare information nicely. Pictographs are attention-getting bar charts but are less accurate. Pie charts show relationships within a whole and statistical maps show location and quantity relationships.

_____   _____   7. During effective automated conferences, one person serves as the moderator to keep the subject on track, the number of participants is of a manageable size, a copy of the agenda has been e-mailed to participants ahead of time, participants say who they are when they speak, and a taped record of the conference is kept.

_____   _____   8. Although video conferencing may seem expensive, it is really very cost effective. It saves employees' time, reduces travel costs, enables more people to participate in decision making, and improves response time for decisions.

(Continued)

Name_____

Interesting   **Uninteresting**

_____   _____   9. Communication technology is the future for fashion merchandising. Information systems will locate, gather, process, and utilize retailing and trend forecasting information for precise decision making.

_____   _____   10. "Broadband" enables users to view large files, such as video, audio, photos, and 3D sent via the Internet. Broadband capability is governed by the "last mile issue," or the connection between the Internet service provider and user, and is important to fashion merchandising businesses.

_____   _____   11. During economic slowdowns, companies cut back on spending, especially on investments in information technology. As retailers sell less and apparel manufacturers produce lower quantities, they make fewer computer system purchases.

_____   _____   12. The term *malware* is short for "malicious software," which disrupts computer operations, gathers sensitive financial or business information, or gains access to private or government computer systems. It includes computer viruses, worms, spyware, adware, and other damaging or disabling computer programs. Some malware might be packed with additional tracking software to gather marketing statistics. Malware has caused the rise in antivirus software and firewalls for protection.

The most interesting statement is #_____ because

_____

_____

_____

_____

_____

_____

_____

Communication Technology Quiz

Activity D   Name _____

Chapter 17   Date _____ Period_____

Write one true/false question for each of the chapter sections noted, and write the correct answers on another piece of paper. If your question is false, write the sentence correctly (true) on your other piece of paper. Then exchange workbook pages with a classmate to try to answer each other's questions correctly. Check answers with the prepared answer sheet.

True or False

Technology for Information Management:

_____ 1. _____

_____

_____

_____

Automated Conferencing, Figure 17-18:

_____ 2. _____

_____

_____

_____

Electronic Retailing:

_____ 3. _____

_____

_____

_____

Communication via Mobile Devices:

_____ 4. _____

_____

_____

_____

Social Media Communications:

_____ 5. _____

_____

_____

_____

(Continued)

Name _____

Going Deeper with Technology:

_____ 6. _____

                 _____

                 _____

                 _____

Analytics:

_____ 7. _____

                 _____

                 _____

                 _____

Retail Applications for Communication Technology:

_____ 8. _____

                 _____

                 _____

                 _____

Communication Match

Activity E	Name _____
Chapter 17	Date _____ Period_____

Match the following terms and definitions by placing the correct letter next to each number.

_____ 1. Websites on which users record experiences, observations, opinions, and information on a regular basis.

_____ 2. Simultaneous communication between geographically dispersed people via audio, video, or computer.

_____ 3. Cellular telephones with built-in applications and Internet access.

_____ 4. Websites that collect and organize content from all over the Internet to help users request and find information and sources.

_____ 5. Levels of responsibility within a company's structure, usually shown on an organization chart.

_____ 6. Homemade videos produced and shown on the Internet by shoppers who share their purchase choices and opinions of the goods.

_____ 7. The sending, storing, and receiving of messages via computers to electronic mailboxes.

_____ 8. Identifying a person's physical location with data obtained from smartphones and other personal GPS-enabled devices.

_____ 9. Two-dimensional matrix bar codes to be scanned with the camera of a mobile device to link consumers to web or mobile sites.

_____ 10. Data sent from a website and stored in users' browsers while they navigate websites and then automatically retrieved when the website is visited again.

_____ 11. One seamless combination of all selling venues together, with the same products and services uniformly offered through the process.

_____ 12. Numbers, statistics, facts, and figures.

_____ 13. The use of computers to draw or chart.

_____ 14. The ability to access information electronically and to allow others who are approved and permitted to access the information.

_____ 15. In communication, instructional display items that appeal mainly to people's vision.

_____ 16. The sending and receiving of messages without using words.

_____ 17. Wireless RFID technologies for smartphones, tablets, and similar devices with 2-way communication to other such devices within close proximity.

A. active listening
B. analytics
C. artificial intelligence (AI)
D. automated conferencing
E. blogs
F. clienteling
G. cloud computing
H. computer graphics
I. conversion rate
J. data
K. electronic mail (e-mail)
L. encoding
M. geotracking
N. haul videos
O. information technology (IT)
P. lines of authority
Q. live chat
R. m-commerce
S. near field communication
T. neural computing
U. nonverbal communication
V. omni-channel retailing
W. open-ended questions
X. organization chart
Y. QR codes
Z. search engines
AA. smartphones
BB. social media
CC. verbal communication
DD. visual aids
EE. web cookies

(Continued)

Name_____

_____ 18. Communication when a shopper and an agent type questions and answers into an instant-message-type box appearing in the consumer's web browser.

_____ 19. The use of electronic programs that can learn internally from their previous activities.

_____ 20. The asking of open-ended questions, thinking about the replies and then asking more questions to probe more deeply and clarify confusing points.

_____ 21. Personal content created and spread via electronic technology for interaction and sharing of information.

_____ 22. The proportion of Internet shoppers who turn into buyers instead of abandoning their carts or clicking off a retail website.

_____ 23. The process of a message sender putting thoughts into symbolic form to be meaningful for the receiver.

_____ 24. A diagram or visual representation of a company's official structure, indicating lines of authority.

_____ 25. Computer systems that display behavior that would be regarded as intelligent if it was observed in humans.

_____ 26. Departments in corporations and independent consultants that specialize in computer communications.

_____ 27. Questions that require multiple-word answers, rather than a yes or no.

_____ 28. The discovery and communication of meaningful patterns in data, using statistics and mathematics.

_____ 29. Wireless mobile selling and buying via such devices as smartphones and tablets.

_____ 30. The effort to increase sales and improve consumers' shopping experiences by collecting and using data about individuals, collected as customers research products digitally and make purchases over time.

_____ 31. Sending messages with the use of words.

Concepts for Successful Selling

Working with Garment Labels

Activity A　　　　　　Name _____

Chapter 18　　　　　　Date _____ Period _____

Study the permanent labels on two different garments and fill in this chart with your findings. Then answer the questions on the back of this page.

Information to provide	Garment A	Garment B
Brief description of the garment		
Location of the label(s) in the garment		
Brief description of the label(s)		
Fiber content of the garment (generic names)		
Percentages of fibers in garment		
Identity of responsible party (RN)		
Country of origin		
Permanent care requirements		
Extra voluntary information (size, fabric structure, special finishes, etc.)		

(Continued)

Name_____

Pretend you are a retailer selling the garments to consumers and respond to the following:

1. After reviewing fiber advantages and disadvantages described in Chapter 6 of the text, what good points might you tell customers about the fiber content of each garment?

Garment A	Garment B

2. What disadvantages might you discuss with customers about the fiber content of each garment?

Garment A	Garment B

3. With knowledge gained from previous chapters, what might you discuss with customers about the country of origin of each garment?

Garment A	Garment B

4. What might you discuss with customers about the care of each garment?

Garment A	Garment B

5. What might you discuss with customers about the extra voluntary information on each label?

Garment A	Garment B

Discussing Selling Skills

Activity B   Name _____

Chapter 18   Date _____ Period_____

In small groups, or as a whole class, discuss the following statements:

1. "Good" retail salespeople often keep the selling floor orderly, have complete merchandise knowledge, and can present goods well to customers. However, they don't know how to close the sale.

2. Some salespeople lose sales because they "prequalify" the customers by their looks, as well as expressing their own opinions too strongly.

3. In the future, stores might take advantage of new technology for "micro-checkout" areas (with smaller amounts of space allotted to cash/wrap activities) or portable POS devices, which will give them higher productivity by increasing their selling space.

4. Effective communication skills of listening actively and adapting to the needs of various customers is often more important for salespeople than tightly following the procedure of making a sale.

5. Salespeople often feel that incentive programs for higher sales are frustrating because they are already doing their best and haven't been educated or trained to sell any better.

6. It is important for salespeople to have and try to maintain a sense of humor.

7. Surveys of retail salespeople have indicated that some sales associates fear customers, while others are so bored in their jobs that they don't try to make sales.

8. Some salespeople feel guilty doing suggestion selling, or recommending add-ons or trade-ups.

9. Retail management should develop a relationship with the company's salespeople, communicate what is expected of them, monitor their activities, and reward their results.

10. Since it is difficult to hire good salespeople, companies might first hire good people and then provide initial and ongoing training about how to sell their goods to their target market.

11. When selling merchandise, salespeople should place their strongest selling points at the beginning (opening) and the end (closing) of their sales communications, rather than in the middle.

12. If it's not out on the floor (displayed for customers to see and buy), it might as well be out of stock.

Choose one statement and express your opinion about it.

_____

_____

_____

_____

_____

_____

_____

Role-Playing to Make Sales

Activity C   **Name** _____

Chapter 18   **Date** _____ **Period** _____

Join with another student in your class and pick one of the following selling situations to role-play in front of the class. One of you will be the retail salesperson and the other will be the customer. Write the main points you will make at the bottom of this page. After your "performance," obtain feedback from classmates about other ways of handling your particular situation.

1. Role-play a sales-oriented (product) approach to selling a particular garment, followed by a customer-oriented sales approach with the same garment.

2. Role-play at least four different sales approaches and greetings to customers for different situations.

3. Role-play the following types of customers and how they should be treated by a salesperson: casual looker, undecided customer, decided customer.

4. Stress features of a particular garment to a customer, especially related to benefits and solutions for that customer.

5. Voice specific objections about a garment and show how the objections might be overcome or changed to advantage.

6. With a basic garment, role-play suggestion selling examples that involve add-ons, trading up, more than one, and special offers.

7. Role-play a preselling telephone call by a salesperson, with the uninterested customer finally being convinced to visit the store for particular reasons.

Main points to be covered:

_____

_____

_____

_____

_____

_____

_____

_____

_____

_____

_____

_____

_____

Techniques for Closing the Sale

Activity D

Chapter 18

Name _____

Date _____ Period_____

After reading the sale closing techniques in the table, fill in the right-hand column with your own examples. Then answer the questions that follow.

Closing technique	Explanation	Given example	Your example
Direct close	The salesperson directly asks the customer for the order.	"May I write this order up for you?"	
Assumptive close	Assuming the customer is going to buy, the salesperson proceeds with completing the sales transaction.	"Would you like to have this gift wrapped?"	
Alternative close	The salesperson asks the customer to make a choice, with either alternative being favorable to the retailer.	"Will this be cash or charge?"	
Sum and agree close	The salesperson summarizes the major features, benefits, and advantages of the products and obtains an affirmative agreement from the customer on each point.	"This suit has the features you were looking for" (yes), "you want the alterations we offer" (yes), "and it is in your price range" (yes). "Let's write up the sale."	
Balance sheet close	The salesperson lists the advantages and disadvantages of making the purchase, and closes by pointing out how the advantages outweigh the disadvantages.	"This suit is on sale, it has all the features you were looking for, you have 90 days to pay for it without any finance charges, and we will take care of the alterations. Even though it can't be ready until next week, now is the time to buy."	

(Continued)

Name _____

Closing technique	Explanation	Given example	Your example
Emotional close	The salesperson appeal to the customer's emotions of love, fear, acceptance, recognition, success, etc.	"Your promotion and raise might well depend on wearing this suit for your big presentation to management."	
Act now close	The salesperson tries to get the customer to act immediately by stressing that the offer is limited.	"The sale ends today and this is the last one we have in stock."	

What closing technique do you feel would work best for small accessory items? Why? _____

_____

_____

_____

_____

_____

What closing technique do you feel would work best for an expensive winter coat? Why? _____

_____

_____

_____

_____

_____

If you were employed by a retailer to sell some type of fashion goods, which technique would you feel comfortable using most of the time? Why? _____

_____

_____

_____

_____

_____

Selling Terms Fill-in-the-Blanks

Activity E   **Name** _____

Chapter 18   **Date** _____ **Period** _____

Complete the following statements by filling in the blanks.

1. Prizes or rewards meant to stimulate people to do better work toward achieving results are known as _____.

2. _____ includes payment and benefits for work accomplished.

3. Nonpersonal promotion aimed at the public or a large general audience is _____ _____.

4. A _____ _____ is a salesperson's questions to a customer to get an indication of what needs to be done to close the sale.

5. A certificate that entitles the customer to buy an out-of-stock advertised special at a later time at the same advertised price is a _____ _____.

6. _____ _____ are salespersons' books of customers' names, addresses, phone numbers, sizes, and important dates.

7. Wholesalers that sell specialized goods, especially through self-service retailers, where they provide, set up, mark prices, and maintain the fixtures for their product lines are called _____ _____.

8. A company's _____ _____ includes the feeling that employees have about their opportunities, value, and rewards for good performance.

9. Responding to the customer's presence, rather than going out to find customers is _____ _____.

10. A _____ _____ is a "cash on delivery" sale that is sent to the customer, with payment made through the delivery company.

11. The _____ _____-_____ feature of computerized point-of-sale systems automatically adjusts prices to the correct amount when bar codes are scanned at check-out.

12. _____-_____ are additional merchandise items, such as related items to create complete outfits.

13. _____ are favorable outcomes received from products.

14. Projected volumes of unit or dollar sales that are assigned to a selling department or person for a certain time period are _____ _____.

15. _____ _____, sometimes called personal selling, is the exchange of merchandise to individual consumers in return for money or credit.

16. A deferred purchase arrangement in which the store sets aside a customer's merchandise until the customer has fully paid for it is called _____.

17. _____ _____ is obtaining larger sales by selling higher-priced, better-quality merchandise to customers.

(Continued)

Name _____

18. A _____ payment to a hired salesperson is based on a percentage of the dollar amount of sales made by that person.

19. To _____ is to search for customers who have the willingness to buy and the ability to pay for the company's products.

20. The merchandising function that includes receiving, preparing, protecting against damage or theft, and controlling the merchandise before it is sold is called _____.

21. _____ are small pieces of ribbon permanently attached in garments or stamped areas on the inside of garments that contain printed information.

22. _____ _____ _____ are goods that are shipped back to a supplier by a store.

23. Increasing sales by adding to the customer's original purchases is

    _____ _____.

24. _____ _____ is an extra percentage of a purchase collected by retailers in most states to be paid to the state government.

25. The stockkeeping function of _____ includes the physical exchange of goods between the vendor's transporting agent to the retailer, as well as inspecting, verifying, and "logging in" the goods.

26. The _____ that products provide are answers to problems.

27. Detachable heavy paper "signs" that are affixed to the outside of garments as a form of promotion to help sell products are called _____.

28. The covering, wrapper, or container in which some merchandise is placed is called

    _____.

Calculating Financial Results

Working with the Operating Statement

Activity A   Name _____

Chapter 19   Date _____ Period_____

After reviewing information about operating statements in the text and reading the following cases, answer the questions that follow. Show equations and your work when possible, using another piece of paper if more space is needed. You may use a calculator if desired.

The Boutique Gift Shop bought a total of $58,000 worth of items to sell in the store during the year. It was a new store and had no beginning inventory, plus there were no returns or allowances during the year. For the year, 100 items sold at $87 each, 150 items sold at $75 each, 300 items sold at $60 each, 450 items sold at $45 each, 600 items sold at $38 each, 800 items sold at $25 each, and 700 items sold at a clearance sale price of $10 each. Sam, the sole proprietor of the small shop, paid $12,000 in rent, $1,800 in utility bills, and paid $1,200 of other miscellaneous expenses. He took the net profit as his salary, from which he then paid taxes.

1. What were the annual sales for the Boutique Gift Shop?

2. What was the cost of goods sold (COGS) for the year?

3. What was the gross margin for the store for the year?

4. What were the shop's operating expenses, before Sam took his salary?

(Continued)

Name_____

5. What is the net profit before taxes, which Sam took as his salary?

6. What if Sam's operating expenses had been a higher amount than the gross margin?

Sam's twin sister, Susan, has an identical store in another town, but she has had it for several years. Her Boutique of Gifts started the year with $5,000 worth of inventory (at cost) and ordered exactly the same merchandise as Sam did for his store. In fact, she was amazed that her sales were identical to Sam's! However, she ended the year with a different $5,000 worth of inventory than she started with. Also, she had $400 worth of returns and allowances during the year, had the same expenses as Sam, but paid herself a salary of $3,000 per month rather than waiting to see what the net profit would be at the end of the year.

7. Write out an operating statement for Susan's store.

8. What two factors caused Susan to have a loss for her business compared to Sam's profit?

Doing Comparative Analysis

Activity B   **Name** _____

Chapter 19   **Date** _____ **Period**_____

After reviewing information about comparative analysis in the text and reading the following case, answer the questions that follow. Show equations and your work when possible, using another piece of paper if more space is needed. You may use a calculator if desired. Round off numbers where needed.

Bargain Department Store had $75,000,000 of net sales last year and will have $80,000,000 of net sales this year. The cost of the merchandise it sold was $48,000,000 last year and will be $52,000,000 this year. The company has held its total expenses at $20,000,000 this year, the same as last year.

1. What is the cost of goods sold ratio for both last year and this year?

2. What is the expense ratio for both last year and this year?

3. Show the operating ratios as percentages along the main categories of an operating statement, subtracting to lead to the gross margin and profit margin for both years.

(Continued)

Name_____

4. Check the gross margin ratio for both years of the chart with a calculation of the numerical equation.

5. Check the profit margin of the chart with its numerical equation for both years.

6. Calculate the annual sales per square foot for a retail store of 20,000 square feet that had annual net sales of $5,500,000.

7. A company is planning to put 16 new stores into major malls, with apparel that averages $300 per square foot of selling space. Its stores will all have selling space that is 90 feet deep and 50 feet wide. What estimates can be made for annual sales of each store and of all the stores combined?

8. Calculate the gross margin return on selling space of the stores in the previous problem if the gross margin for each store is expected to be $94,500.

9. On another piece of paper, write word problems for a classmate to calculate a store's average sales per hour, average items per transaction, and average dollars per transaction.

Calculating Differences

Activity C   **Name** _____

Chapter 19   **Date** _____ **Period**_____

In relation to this chapter, what is the difference between:

1. Operating statement and income statement? _____

   _____

   _____

   _____

   _____

2. Gross sales and net sales? _____

   _____

   _____

   _____

   _____

3. Cost of goods sold (COGS) and expense management? _____

   _____

   _____

   _____

   _____

4. Gross margin and profit margin? _____

   _____

   _____

   _____

   _____

5. Comparative analysis and operating ratios? _____

   _____

   _____

   _____

   _____

6. Net profit and profitability range? _____

   _____

   _____

   _____

   _____

(Continued)

Name _____

7. Sales per square foot and sales productivity? _____

_____

_____

_____

_____

8. Same-store sales growth and comparable-store sales? _____

_____

_____

_____

_____

9. Fixed costs and variable costs? _____

_____

_____

_____

_____

10. Odd-figure pricing and loss leaders? _____

_____

_____

_____

_____

11. Markup and keystone markup? _____

_____

_____

_____

_____

12. Initial markup and maintained markup? _____

_____

_____

_____

_____

13. Elastic demand and inelastic demand? _____

_____

_____

_____

Discussing Retail Finances

Activity D   Name _____

Chapter 19   Date _____ Period_____

Read the following statements. Then react to each statement or write a comment about it. Finally, in small groups, or as a whole class, discuss the statements, using your comments to contribute to the discussion.

1. After merchandise, labor costs make up retailers' largest expense item. This is followed by energy costs that include lights, heating, and air conditioning.

   _____

   _____

   _____

2. Financial statements indicate where companies have been in the past. Performance indicators show predictions of where they think they are going in the future.

   _____

   _____

   _____

3. As sales per square foot increase for strong retailers, operating costs as a percentage of sales decline. That translates into lower prices for customers, which boosts sales to even higher sales per square foot. Conversely, weak competitors have declining sales per square foot, which leads to rising operating costs as a percentage of sales. They then have problems keeping prices competitive or offering amenities that keep customers happy.

   _____

   _____

   _____

4. Retailers always watch the government's tax reform movements. Lower income taxes for the general population would boost sales, since consumers would have more money to spend. On the other hand, retailers feel that a national consumption (sales) tax would hurt their businesses because consumers would pay more taxes every time they made more purchases.

   _____

   _____

   _____

5. Retailers prefer to stock their stores with merchandise lines that regularly "sell-through" at full price. They try to do "regular price" business whenever they can, but have a suggested "break date" when the goods will go on sale.

   _____

   _____

   _____

(Continued)

Name_____

6. The pricing of private label lines is often done backwards. Instead of buying merchandise available in the market and adding a certain markup, retailers listen to their customers about what they desire and how much they will spend for it. Then product development staffs develop the goods at the desired price points.

_____

_____

_____

_____

7. When retailers donate their unsold apparel goods to certified overseas relief organizations (charity), they not only can receive a full tax deduction on the value, but also a return of any import taxes that were paid on goods produced offshore.

_____

_____

_____

_____

8. For companies that have extremely large numbers listed on their financial statements, three zeros are dropped from all numbers and "(000)" is noted near the top of the statement. That indicates that three zeros should be added to all figures.

_____

_____

_____

_____

9. Rapid fashion shifts can significantly increase regular-price sales and higher profit margins.

_____

_____

_____

_____

10. A policy of "aging" the inventory reduces the temptation for buyers to overbuy because "write-downs" occur that reduce the value of old, unsold stock. When the financial statements are calculated, aged inventory has a lower value that reduces gross profits.

_____

_____

_____

_____

_____

Merchandise Pricing

Activity E Name _____

Chapter 19 Date _____ Period_____

Complete the following exercises and show your work for the problems.

1. What is repricing and why is it done? _____

   _____

   _____

   _____

   _____

2. Figure the markup percent of cost and markup percent of selling price for a coat that costs the store $64 to buy and retails for $114.56.

3. If store policy dictates marking up goods 75% of cost, at what retail selling price should the coat be priced (that cost the store $64)?

4. A certain chain store uses a 40% markup of the selling price. Compute the selling prices for a shirt that cost the store $15 to buy and trousers that cost the store $24.

5. An upscale dress shop uses a 62% markup of the selling price. Compute the separate selling prices for an evening gown that cost the store $152 to buy and a cocktail suit that cost the store $190.

(Continued)

Name _____

6. If a store uses a keystone markup for its pricing, what would the retail price be for a dress that cost the store $48?

7. What does reduction planning involve? _____

_____

_____

_____

8. What is the selling price of an item that had an original ticketed price of $68.95 and was marked down 25%?

9. What is the markdown percentage of the ticketed price of a retail item that was originally priced at $55.50 and sold for $44.95?

10. What would the month's markdown percent be for a store that had $15,300 of markdowns in a month in which the net sales were $102,000?

11. Why is the maintained markup percent the most important indicator of pricing success? _____

_____

_____

_____

12. Calculate the maintained markup percent for a store that uses an original markup of 48% and had an overall markdown of 12% during the period.

Service, Safety, and Security

Customer Service Cases

Activity A   Name _____

Chapter 20   Date _____ Period_____

For each category listed on the left (#1 through 3), circle the word or phrase among the rest that does **not** fit. On the line directly underneath, add one more word or phrase that **does** fit into that category. Then, pretend you are a retail consultant and give good customer service to each of the people described in #4 through 9.

1. Self-Service Retailing: Price positioning   Essential services   Fashion and specialty items   Discount stores

    _____

2. Medium-Service Retailing: Optional services   Value positioning   Selection of goods for comparison   Chain stores

    _____

3. Full-Service Retailing: Service positioning   Specialty boutiques   Convenience items   Upscale department stores

    _____

4. Kadisha has been looking for a red dress for a special Valentine party that is a week away. She has found a perfect dress for the party, but it is only available in green or blue at the branch of the store nearest her home. How might the salesperson give good customer service to Kadisha?

    _____

    _____

    _____

    _____

5. Gloria owns a small dress shop that has not been very profitable lately. She has heard that previous customers have been shopping at a new store that has a fancier interior and offers gift boxes with purchases. What might she do to get these old customers back and attract new ones?

    _____

    _____

    _____

    _____

(Continued)

Name_____

6. The Ritz Department Store has added many customer services, such as a musician playing a harp at the entrance, accepting telephone orders to be delivered to customers, and presenting fashion shows every Saturday afternoon. However, the employees are poorly paid and have not been trained in ways to treat customers properly. What advice would you give to store management and why?

_____

_____

_____

_____

_____

7. Sales volume at the XYZ Department Store is good, but is not increasing, even though housing developments have been going on nearby. Mr. Sinclair, the manager, would like his employees to try to find out about customer satisfaction in several different service categories. How might he do this?

_____

_____

_____

_____

8. John's Menswear Shop is in the center of town. John has been considering relocating the store to the edge of town where he could have his own parking lot, but that move would be very expensive. Parking is free, but scarce, along the street near his current shop, and a parking garage has been built between the alley behind John's store and the next street. What might John do to bring in more customers to his current location instead of moving?

_____

_____

_____

_____

9. The One-Stop Discount Emporium sells merchandise that most people want and is organized so customers can find items easily. However, to keep prices low, the store has only a few checkout cashiers, who must also answer telephone questions and requests. Lately, customers are leaving the checkout areas in bad moods. What might the store do to better satisfy its customers?

_____

_____

_____

_____

Questioning Credit Services

Activity B   **Name** _____

Chapter 20   **Date** _____ **Period**_____

Answer the following questions about credit services.

1. Describe installment credit. _____

   _____

   _____

   _____

   _____

2. Describe proprietary credit cards. _____

   _____

   _____

   _____

   _____

3. How can companies with proprietary credit cards maintain a personal relationship with customers?

   _____

   _____

   _____

   _____

4. What extra operating expenses can occur with proprietary credit card systems? _____

   _____

   _____

   _____

5. Describe private label credit cards. _____

   _____

   _____

   _____

6. What are the two main disadvantages of third-party credit cards? _____

   _____

   _____

   _____

   _____

(Continued)

Name _____

7. Why do secured credit cards tend to generate greater office work and higher costs? _____

_____

_____

_____

_____

8. To what new group of customers does a retailer gain access by offering a secured credit card program? _____

_____

_____

_____

_____

9. Why might secured credit customers be good for stores? _____

_____

_____

_____

_____

10. Why is credit card transaction processing speed sometimes slow? _____

_____

_____

_____

_____

11. Who gets a copy of a multiple-layer credit card slip after the customer has signed it? _____

_____

_____

_____

_____

Group Safety and Security

Activity C   **Name** _____

Chapter 20   **Date** _____ **Period**_____

With a small group of classmates, pick one of the following activities. Present your material to the rest of the class.

A. Develop four different scenarios in which retail customers or employees might be unsafe from crime and/or injury in a retail setting. Ask other students to describe what should be done to minimize or eliminate customer safety hazards.

B. Develop four different scenarios that describe situations of retail external theft. Ask other students to describe what should be done to minimize or eliminate the theft.

C. Develop four different scenarios that describe situations of retail internal theft. Ask other students to describe what should be done to minimize or eliminate the theft.

1. _____

   _____

   _____

   _____

   _____

2. _____

   _____

   _____

   _____

   _____

3. _____

   _____

   _____

   _____

   _____

4. _____

   _____

   _____

   _____

   _____

Service, Safety, and Security Crossword

Activity D   Name _____

Chapter 20   Date _____   Period _____

Complete this crossword puzzle using the clues listed.

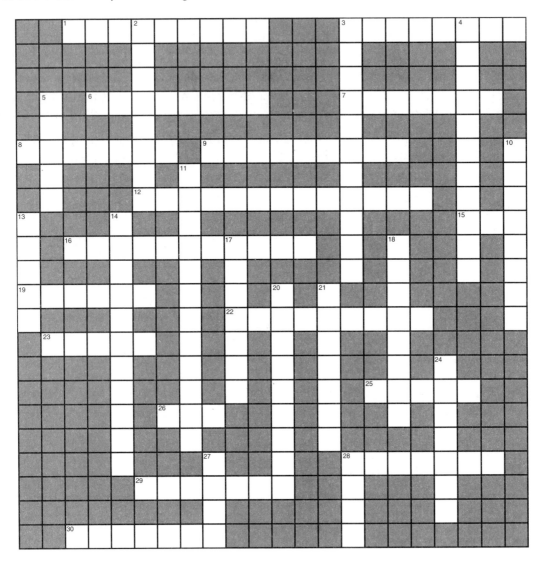

Across

1. _____ is the stealing of a company's inventory or cash in small, petty amounts.
3. _____ involves protection from danger, information loss, fires/catastrophes, and terrorism threats.
6. _____ theft involves stealing by those who are not employed or otherwise associated with a firm.
7. _____ label credit cards are charge cards with the store's name and logo, but issued and managed by a bank.

8. _____ is violent after-hours theft, sometimes called burglary.
9. _____ resolution is the settlement of customers' dissatisfactions with a retailer through mutual agreement as to how to solve specific problems.
12. _____ is cashier activity of providing discounts, uncharged items, or fraudulent returns to friends, relatives, or theft partners.
15. The three letters that stand for a shoplifting prevention system that uses specially-designed

(Continued)

Copyright by The Goodheart-Willcox Co., Inc.

Name_____

tags that contain a small circuit that emits a signal which, if not deactivated, is sensed by devices at exits.

16. _____ credit cards are retail-issued charge cards that are owned, operated, and managed by the retail firm.

19. _____ processing is electronic approval and ongoing authorization of credit transactions.

22. A check _____ is a personal check acceptance program in which the risk falls on the bank/firm that authorizes the transaction.

23. _____ processing takes the money for each purchase directly out of the consumer's bank account and electronically puts it into the merchant's bank account.

25. A _____ positioning customer service strategy offers limited service, mid-price retailing with expected services offered.

26. A flash _____ is a gang that steals large amounts of retail goods quickly.

28. Customer _____ is the total of all enhancements offered to customers, not directly related to the sale of specific products.

29. _____ credit cards are charge cards linked to a savings account containing enough money to back up most or all of the credit line.

30. _____ gift cards can be ordered online and sent immediately via e-mail.

Down

2. Service _____ make up the actual service mix offerings of a company.

3. _____ is the stealing of merchandise from a retail store by a person posing as a customer.

4. An _____ plan is a credit agreement with a small down payment and additional payments spread over several months or years.

5. _____ wrap is putting customer purchases in a distinctive store box, bag, or wrapping paper of a particular color and design.

10. _____ credit is the use of credit cards or other purchase charges that allow consumers to have merchandise immediately and pay for it later.

11. Check _____ is electronic authorization of the probable risk of accepting individual personal checks from customers.

13. A _____ positioning retail strategy of retailing includes self-service, discount retailing with only essential services offered.

14. A service _____ strategy is retailing with a distinctive service mix, often used by specialty stores and upscale department stores.

17. Source _____ is the integration of anti-shoplifting tags into product packaging at the manufacturing level.

18. _____ theft is stealing by employees.

20. _____ parking is a customer service in which the store marks the parking lot/garage stub as paid.

21. _____ is putting merchandise into a sack for better handling, protection, and privacy of customer purchases.

24. Service _____ is how well services are performed to approach, meet, or exceed customer expectations.

27. Stores with salespeople who assist customers one-to-one, in every phase of the shopping process, are _____-service retailers.

28. _____-service retailing is when customers must locate products themselves, compare items, make an unassisted decision, and carry their selections to a checkstand.

Safe and Secure Statements

Activity E   **Name** _____

Chapter 20   **Date** _____ **Period** _____

Write your thoughts about the following statements on the lines, and try to expand the topic further. Use another piece of paper if more space is needed. Then share your thoughts with others by having a class discussion about each statement.

1. According to the National Retail Federation, shoplifting accounts for over $35 billion of estimated losses in America each year. This huge number raises prices for all consumers, in order to compensate for the losses. _____

_____

_____

_____

_____

2. EAS systems are powerful deterrents to shoplifting, but have two drawbacks. First, they do not deter employee theft, which is the major source of shrinkage volume. Second, bad feelings are created when shoppers trigger such systems accidentally—through no fault of their own—and are stopped and questioned. _____

_____

_____

_____

_____

3. New shopper self-checkout devices let customers scan their own purchases with portable scanners to check out faster. The retailer conducts spot-checks to verify customer correctness. However, some customers may not feel comfortable doing the scanning work, spot-checks can detain busy shoppers and imply they are not honest, and unintentional mistakes are humiliating if detected.

_____

_____

_____

_____

4. Some retailers handle customer complaints at a centralized office or complaint desk with trained personnel, a uniform policy, and better feedback to management. Retailers prefer this system. However, customers prefer a decentralized system in which complaints are taken at the department where the purchase was made. _____

_____

_____

_____

_____

(Continued)

Name _____

5. Retail stores have had an increase in bad checks recently, including counterfeit payroll checks. Thus, to reduce check fraud losses, new check acceptance rules include online verification, check guarantee services, inkless fingerprint programs, and tighter account opening policies by banks.

_____

_____

_____

6. Shoplifting "bad stops" of innocent customers by security guards, or thieves who claim innocence after managing to dispose of goods before being stopped and searched, can be costly to retailers. Negative publicity is bad enough, but lawsuits also occur. Therefore, companies are giving more extensive training to their security employees and adopting customer service-oriented strategies aimed at keeping these matters out of court. _____

_____

_____

_____

7. Policies for granting credit are often based on the applicant's "3 C's" which are Character (maturity, honesty), Capacity (earning power, ability to pay), and Capital (assets, goods owned). These are determined through personal interviews, reference checks, and the applicant's credit history.

_____

_____

_____

8. There has been a sharp rise in consumer debt rates and bankruptcies in the past few years. Retailers and credit card companies have mounting losses from unpaid accounts. However, now consumers who "load up" on credit purchases just prior to their bankruptcy filing still owe those amounts even after declaring bankruptcy. _____

_____

_____

_____

9. Retailer-owned credit card banks exist only to issue credit cards. These "nonbanks" are set up in a state with advantageous laws. Owning the credit card issuing institution gives retailers income from receivables, complete control over credit, and sole access to transaction data for target marketing purposes. _____

_____

_____

_____

Fashion Promotion Through Advertising and the **Press**

Multiple Fashion Promotion Choices

Activity A

Chapter 21

Name _____

Date _____ Period_____

Write eight multiple choice questions using information from the beginning of the chapter (the major section entitled "Fashion Promotion" that ends with "Promotion Ethics"). Record the letters of the correct answers on another piece of paper. Then exchange questions with a classmate to try to answer each other's questions correctly.

1. _____

   _____

   a. _____

   b. _____

   c. _____

   d. _____

2. _____

   _____

   a. _____

   b. _____

   c. _____

   d. _____

3. _____

   _____

   a. _____

   b. _____

   c. _____

   d. _____

(Continued)

Name_____

4. _____

_____

a. _____

b. _____

c. _____

d. _____

5. _____

_____

a. _____

b. _____

c. _____

d. _____

6. _____

_____

a. _____

b. _____

c. _____

d. _____

7. _____

_____

a. _____

b. _____

c. _____

d. _____

8. _____

_____

a. _____

b. _____

c. _____

d. _____

Advertising Questions

Activity B   **Name** _____

Chapter 21   **Date** _____ **Period** _____

Answer the following questions about advertising.

1. What category of stores does the most advertising of all retailers? _____

   _____

   _____

2. What does advocacy advertising try to do? _____

   _____

   _____

3. What types of companies sponsor national advertising and local advertising, respectively? _____

   _____

   _____

4. What relationship should the timing of ads have with merchandise availability? _____

   _____

   _____

5. What is the right media to use for advertising? _____

   _____

   _____

   _____

6. Name three print media forms and two broadcast media forms. _____

   _____

   _____

   _____

   _____

7. Why have newspapers decreased in favor for local retail ads? _____

   _____

   _____

8. What are infomercials? _____

   _____

   _____

9. What are tabloid inserts? _____

   _____

   _____

(Continued)

Name_____

10. Instead of advertising in expensive large city daily newspapers, what might be a better value for the ads of small retailers? _____

_____

_____

11. Name three examples of outdoor advertising. _____

_____

_____

_____

12. Name three examples of direct mail advertising. _____

_____

_____

_____

13. What type of retailers often use direct mail advertising? _____

_____

_____

14. Why is it often hard to communicate fashion or style-trend messages with radio ads? _____

_____

_____

15. What is the key to having radio messages remembered? _____

_____

_____

16. Why are fashion ads and home shopping sales effective on television? _____

_____

_____

17. What is the headline of an advertisement? _____

_____

_____

18. What does the layout of a print advertisement do? _____

_____

_____

Analyzing a Fashion Ad

Activity C   **Name** _____

Chapter 21   **Date** _____ **Period**_____

Study print advertising in current fashion publications. Then cut out a fashion advertisement, mount it here, and analyze it according to the following questions.

1. What trend is being promoted? _____

_____

_____

_____

2. What is the target audience for the ad? _____

_____

_____

_____

3. What image is presented by the ad? _____

_____

_____

_____

4. Does the ad quickly get the reader's attention? _____

_____

_____

_____

5. Does the ad keep the reader's attention? _____

_____

_____

(Continued)

Name_____

6. Are all the elements of an ad included? _____

_____

_____

7. Is the information presented from the customer's viewpoint? _____

_____

_____

8. Does the ad have a single recognizable theme, and what is it? _____

_____

_____

_____

_____

9. Is the product shown and described as the customer would use it, and how? _____

_____

_____

_____

_____

_____

10. Is the location where the product is available clearly indicated, possibly more than once? _____

_____

_____

_____

11. Is there a request for action by the customer? Explain. _____

_____

_____

_____

_____

_____

12. Overall, how effective do you think the ad is? Why? _____

_____

_____

_____

Promotion Terms Matching

Activity D   Name _____

Chapter 21   Date _____ Period_____

Match the following terms and definitions by placing the correct letter next to each number.

_____ 1. Promotional messages used to correct previous false or unethical claims.

_____ 2. Advertising designed to sell specific, identifiable merchandise items, lines, or services, to get an immediate response.

_____ 3. A promotional collection of materials presented as a portfolio with press releases and photographs and/or illustrations.

_____ 4. Any paid form of nonpersonal sales message, made by an identified sponsor, through a mass communication.

_____ 5. Unpaid media coverage of news about an organization or its products and activities, presented at the discretion of the media.

_____ 6. Promotion directly to consumers, usually by companies that do not sell directly to consumers.

_____ 7. Acting or dealing in good morally evaluated ways.

_____ 8. Promotion aimed within the industry, to the next segment of the distribution chain, stressing how well the product performs and the projected profits if purchased.

_____ 9. The specific media form(s) chosen or combined for an advertising campaign.

_____ 10. Mention in a publication of a manufacturer's tradename, or specific retail sources for merchandise featured by the publication.

_____ 11. Activities that try to build good relations with the various publics of an organization or product line.

_____ 12. Types of media available for advertising.

_____ 13. Service firms that provide advertising expertise, and design, produce, and place ads in the media.

_____ 14. Image or corporate advertising designed to sell public awareness and organization reputation, rather than specific products.

_____ 15. A written guide that details the company's promotion efforts for a certain period of time, as well as for single important events.

A. advertising
B. advertising agencies
C. advertising platform
D. consumer promotion
E. corrective advertising
F. editorial credit
G. endorsements
H. ethics
I. inbound marketing
J. infographics
K. institutional advertising
L. media forms
M. media vehicle
N. outbound marketing
O. press kit
P. press release
Q. product advertising
R. promotion mix
S. promotion program
T. publicity
U. public relations
V. retail promotion
W. sponsor
X. trade promotion
Y. word-of-mouth advertising
Z. worldwide advertising

(Continued)

Name_____

_____ 16. A written "news" story sent as publicity to newspapers and magazines.

_____ 17. The combination of all types of persuasive communication used by an organization to market itself and influence the purchase of merchandise.

_____ 18. Promotion by a store to its customers.

_____ 19. The company that pays for an advertisement.

_____ 20. A plan that defines the target audience and summarizes the audience-pleasing benefits and features of the product for an advertising campaign.

_____ 21. The combination of visual design and data, minimizing words to explain concepts.

_____ 22. The practice of companies sending out marketing messages.

_____ 23. Testimonials of famous people to vouch for products.

_____ 24. The scope of sales messages sent via the Internet.

_____ 25. People telling others of their experiences with retailers and other companies.

_____ 26. Having consumers seek out and find a company and its merchandise electronically.

Group Promotion Activities

Activity E   Name _____

Chapter 21   Date _____ Period_____

Working in a small group, do one of the following activities. Then present your material to the rest of the class. When you are finished, allow classmates to ask questions or give constructive criticism.

   A. Study the fashion promotion programs of several stores by noting their events, displays, advertising, etc. Then develop a fashion promotion program for a fictional retailer. Prepare a promotion calendar for the retailer and coordinate advertising with it. Consider store goals and image, coordination of advertising with fashion seasons and sales activities, and where and when to use promotion activities and advertising. Although you won't have an actual budget, try to plan the most effective program for the least amount of money.

   B. Create a sale flyer for a specific type of store. Decide on a target market and a product line to promote. Create a rough draft before preparing the final version. It should be neat and easy to read, have correct grammar and spelling, be creative and original, and appropriate for the type of store. It must include the store name/address/hours, item(s) for sale and price, and date(s) of availability or special pricing. With the main goal of selling merchandise, you may include a slogan, theme, special offer, or other sales tactic.

   C. Evaluate the nonprint advertising of several retailers. Then plan the nonprint media mix that maximizes the selling ability of a fictitious store. As part of the mix, create a television advertisement with video equipment, and/or a radio advertisement with audio equipment. Explain your advertising plan and play your production(s) for the class.

   D. Analyze a selection of fashion magazines. For each, explain to the class the image of the magazine, type of audience, size of readership, amount and kinds of ads it carries, cost of each size ad, and why advertisers may choose each magazine. The size of readership and cost of advertising is available by calling the advertising number on the title page. Also note the types of fashion news/trend articles and how each magazine is different as well as similar to the others.

Letter of the activity chosen: _____

Names of those in the group and their assignments for this project:

_____

_____

_____

_____

_____

Overall evaluation of the project:

_____

_____

_____

Visual Merchandising

Visual Merchandising Outline

Activity A

Chapter 22

Name _____

Date _____ Period_____

Before studying Chapter 22, slowly page through the textbook and outline the chapter on this form. Write section titles on the lines to go with the printed explanations. Then, after reviewing the outline titles and their meanings, explain which section of the chapter you think will be the most interesting to you and why.

I. _____ of Visual Merchandising.

II. The _____—The inside of the store.

    A. _____—Arrangement of store sales areas planned to use space effectively, with maximum flexibility for merchandise and display changes.

    B. _____—A decorating theme carried throughout the store to fit with the company's image and create a particular emotional mood.

III. _____—Arrangement of goods in a retail store that attempts to show the complete assortment.

    A. _____—Equipment that holds merchandise for sale, coordinated with the retailer's merchandise style, inventory level, and budget.

    B. _____—Goods shown on side barriers of selling areas that draw customers farther into the store.

IV. _____—Showings of products as attention-getting focal points inside a store.

    A. _____—Parts of visual merchandise presentations.

        1. _____—The central focus of apparel/accessory displays.

        2. _____—Illumination used to direct customers' attention to displays.

        3. _____—Extra items that reinforce the themes of displays.

        4. _____—Placards or other signs that inform shoppers.

    B. _____—Formulating store display ideas according to the number of items available, season of the year, what has been displayed recently, and planned advertising.

(Continued)

Name _____

V. _____—Showings of products to be seen from the outside of the store.

   A. _____—Benefits and drawbacks of window displays.

   B. _____—The various kinds of visual presentations to be seen from the outside of the store.

      1. _____—Displays that have a full background and sides that completely separate the store's interior from the display window.

      2. _____—Displays with a partial background that shuts out some of the store interior from viewers outside the store.

      3. _____—Window displays with no background panel so the entire store is visible to passersby through them.

      4. _____—Four-sided display windows that stand alone, often in lobbies.

VI. _____—Mail-order and website display.

The section of the chapter that I think will be the most interesting to me is _____ because

_____

_____

_____

_____

_____

_____

_____

_____

_____

_____

_____

_____

_____

_____

_____

_____

_____

_____

_____

_____

Visual Merchandising Match

Activity B   **Name** _____

Chapter 22   **Date** _____ **Period** _____

Match the following terms and definitions by placing the correct letter next to each number.

_____ 1. The ways that goods are hung, placed on shelves, or otherwise made available for sale in retail stores.

_____ 2. A free-flowing floor plan arrangement with fixtures in informal, unbalanced placements.

_____ 3. Merchandise presentation fixtures that stock small amounts of merchandise that face outward toward shoppers.

_____ 4. A retail floor plan with one or more primary aisles running through the store and secondary aisles intersecting with them at right angles.

_____ 5. A drawing showing the arrangement of physical space, such as the positioning of merchandise groups and customer services for a retail store.

_____ 6. Shelves, tables, rods, counters, stands, easels, forms, and platforms on which merchandise is stocked and displayed for sale.

_____ 7. Life-like human forms.

_____ 8. The face-out presentation of apparel merchandise by hanging with the front fully facing the viewer.

_____ 9. Lighting that focuses attention on specific areas or targeted items of merchandise.

_____ 10. Store layout areas where merchandise is displayed and customers interact with sales personnel.

_____ 11. Light directed over an entire wide display area with recessed ceiling lights.

_____ 12. A way of hanging garments, with only one side showing from shoulder to bottom.

_____ 13. Lighting that focuses a narrow beam on a specific merchandise item on display.

_____ 14. Store spaces devoted to customer services, merchandise receiving and distribution, management offices, and staff activities.

_____ 15. Added objects that support the theme of a display.

_____ 16. "Slant arm" merchandise fixtures intended to hold one item per knob.

A. atmospherics
B. beamspread
C. capacity fixtures
D. décor
E. displays
F. face-forward
G. feature fixtures
H. fixtures (retail)
I. floodlighting
J. grid layout
K. mannequins
L. maze layout
M. merchandise presentation
N. pinpointing (lighting)
O. planogram
P. props (display)
Q. sales support areas
R. selling areas
S. shoulder out
T. signage
U. spotlighting
V. store layout
W. visual merchandising
X. wall standards
Y. waterfalls (display)

(Continued)

Name _____

_____ 17. Vertical strips used on walls, with holes into which all types of brackets and fixtures can be inserted.

_____ 18. Merchandise presentation fixtures that stock large amounts of merchandise.

_____ 19. The interior arrangement of retail facilities.

_____ 20. Individual, special, visual presentations of merchandise.

_____ 21. The style and appearance of interior furnishings.

_____ 22. The physical presentation of goods in the most attractive and understandable ways, to increase sales.

_____ 23. The diameter of the circle of light created by a light source.

_____ 24. Features, such as sound and smell, intended to create a particular emotional mood or attitude.

_____ 25. Individual letters and complete information plaques to inform viewers.

Visual Merchandising Truths and Myths

Activity C   Name _____

Chapter 22   Date _____ Period_____

After reading each of the following statements, indicate if you think the statement is a myth or a truth by checking the appropriate column. Then turn to the back of this page to check your answers. Later, discuss the statements as a class.

	Myth	**Truth**
1. Mall owners often seek out tenants that have attractive décor and displays to attract customers.	_____	_____
2. After entering a store, shoppers tend to turn left, and about half of them go all the way to the back of the store.	_____	_____
3. Visual merchandising has been called "theater of merchandise" because it is the purposeful staging of goods for an audience.	_____	_____
4. Many display fixtures now are on locking wheels, for mobility of space use. Store employees can reconfigure a department overnight.	_____	_____
5. Opportunities for window displays have increased, while the importance of store layout/décor and interior merchandise displays have decreased.	_____	_____
6. Some of the most interesting display props are "found" items from flea markets that must be refurbished before being used.	_____	_____
7. A display "vignette" shows multiple merchandise items that have no common theme, except that they are all sold in the store/department.	_____	_____
8. New mannequins for feature displays are inexpensive and are stylish for about six years.	_____	_____
9. The attention of passersby can be drawn and held to displays with contrast, repetition, physical motion, and lighting.	_____	_____
10. "Concept shops" have become popular lately, with entire departments or stores based around strong themes or lifestyle images.	_____	_____
11. Customers of multilevel department stores often think of the basement for bargains and the top floor for exclusive designer goods.	_____	_____
12. "Proscenium" is an ornate arch or valance along the top and sides of window displays that hides the lighting, separates windows or display groupings, and/or forms a decorative frame for the window.	_____	_____
13. In an effort to cut costs, retailers are dimming their lights. This also makes merchandise colors look more appealing than they really are in true sunlight.	_____	_____
14. Although computer technology is good for calculations involving many retail tasks, merchandise display work can only really be planned and evaluated as the work is actually done on the sales floor.	_____	_____
15. Besides the grid and maze layouts, stores sometimes arrange the sales floor into a boutique layout, with individual, separated retail areas. The areas have different shopping themes and resemble small specialty shops.	_____	_____

(Continued)

Name _____

1. *Truth.* To create an exciting atmosphere for shoppers throughout the mall, which also enables mall owners to charge higher rents to tenants; the types of décor and displays of prospective tenants is a prime consideration when filling available spaces.

2. *Myth.* Shoppers tend to turn right when they enter, which should be considered when allocating space to various merchandise departments. Also, only about one-quarter of the shoppers go more than halfway into the store. Displayed goods are important to pique their interest.

3. *Truth.* Employees who create a store's displays are more successful if they consider their work as visual "productions." They must use lights, props, and other theater elements effectively, and enable the "actors" (merchandise items) to shine for an audience of shoppers.

4. *Truth.* New display fixtures are more mobile than in the past, giving more flexibility to all arrangements of merchandise presentation tables, shelves, hangers, and mannequins.

5. *Myth.* Just the opposite—there are fewer retail windows in which to place displays these days, so the importance of store layout/décor and interior merchandise displays has increased.

6. *Truth.* Small stores often use unusual old furniture, plant stands, or other interesting "attic" items found by the owner or display manager. Large stores have more conventional props, unless they outsource their work to a display service that has a warehouse of "collectibles."

7. *Myth.* A display "vignette" creates a realistic atmosphere that suggests that an activity is actually going on or that people are really doing something—like a picture or movie frame.

8. *Myth.* New mannequins cost hundreds of dollars and are stylish for only about half that amount of time (three years). Inexpensive mannequins usually look cheap and have stilted poses. Thus, alternative ways to display goods are often used.

9. *Truth.* The same methods can be used to draw attention to displays as are used for emphasis in clothing, leading to harmony as studied with design elements and principles in Chapter 8.

10. *Truth.* Concept shops have their décor, merchandise fixtures, and displays strongly associated with particular lifestyles, creating shopping "experiences" that are directly related to the goods.

11. *Truth.* With "bargain basement" and "penthouse" images created over many years, the right floor for merchandise is the one that is most consistent with where customers think things should be and where the retailer can provide the goods and services customers expect.

12. *Truth.* A decorative "proscenium" can accent certain colors or occasions depicted in the window display, or promote storewide events or themes with decorative motifs around the edge of the window.

13. *Myth.* Stores are increasing their light levels because of stricter energy codes mandated by the U.S. Environmental Protection Agency, more lighting options available, the requirements of aging eyes of maturing baby boom customers, and to give a theatrical/entertainment image. With more efficient light sources, most stores are achieving a brighter appearance while also reducing energy costs.

14. *Myth.* New space management software programs can eliminate guesswork with "virtual merchandising" (designing store planograms that show 3-dimensional arrangements). Electronic 3-D planning can create inviting areas for shoppers and maximize space utilization for retailers. Merchandise can be ordered to fit the configurations.

15. *Truth.* Larger stores, that have the space, can create unusual and fun shopping experiences for customers with a boutique layout. Each separate area has its own décor and ambiance that coincides with the merchandise being sold in that area.

Visual Merchandising Facts

Activity D   **Name** _____

Chapter 22   **Date** _____ **Period**_____

Respond to the following about visual merchandising.

1. Besides the main purposes of selling goods and promoting the store image, name at least three specific purposes of visual merchandising. _____

   _____

   _____

   _____

2. With what three factors should an appropriate fixture plan coordinate? _____

   _____

   _____

   _____

3. Name and briefly describe at least four common types of retail fixtures. _____

   _____

   _____

   _____

   _____

4. Name at least four things that displays are intended to do. _____

   _____

   _____

   _____

   _____

5. Name at least three different interior retail display locations. _____

   _____

   _____

   _____

6. Name at least four criteria for selecting particular merchandise items for displays. _____

   _____

   _____

   _____

   _____

(Continued)

Name_____

7. Name and briefly describe at least four of the types of merchandise groupings for displays.

_____

_____

_____

_____

_____

_____

_____

8. Name and briefly describe three beamspread techniques that are often used to create desired effects in displays. _____

_____

_____

_____

_____

_____

_____

9. Name and briefly describe the three main categories of props that are used for displays.

_____

_____

_____

_____

_____

_____

10. Name and briefly describe three variations of enclosed display windows. _____

_____

_____

_____

_____

_____

_____

Becoming Visual Merchandisers

Activity E   Name _____

Chapter 22   Date _____ Period_____

With a group of classmates, pick one of the two following activities. After completing the assignment, present your material to the rest of the class. When you are finished, let classmates ask questions or give additional ideas and comments.

A. Design a planogram for a fashion specialty store in a strip shopping center or mall. After making general decisions about the type of merchandise, image, and target market of the store, decide on the actual dimensions of space for the store. You may want to visit some stores to get an idea of actual square footages (for instance, space that is 60 feet long and 40 feet wide has 60′ × 40′ = 2400 square feet). Individually sketch several arrangements of selling areas and sales support areas. Then, as a group, decide on a final floor plan and draw it in ¼″ scale (in which ¼ inch equals 1 foot). Show the location of specific sales support areas, such as offices, receiving, employee restroom, etc. In the selling area, show merchandise group spaces, fixtures, feature display locations, and the cash/wrap area. Also show fitting rooms and any display windows. Consider aisles and/or open spaces for shopper traffic patterns, as well as visibility for merchandise presentation.

B. Plan an original interior or window display that shows a certain type of fashion apparel to a particular target clientele. Do preliminary sketches as you solidify the ideas for the display, deciding on the theme, merchandise and grouping, props, lighting, signage, etc., that would be needed. You may want to review the elements and principles of design described in Chapter 8 of the text. Draw the final version of the display onto a large poster board or create a scale model. Describe the hypothetical location where the display would be placed, and how the display materials selected would enhance the merchandise. What customer behavior might result from the display?

Letter of the activity chosen: _____

Names of those in the group and their assignments for this activity:

_____

_____

_____

_____

_____

Overall evaluation of the activity:

_____

_____

_____

_____

_____

Special Event Fashion Shows

Fashion Show Planning

Activity A   **Name** _____

Chapter 23   **Date** _____ **Period** _____

Respond to the following questions about planning fashion shows.

1. Who would most likely be the fashion show coordinator for a small apparel shop? _____

   _____

   _____

   _____

2. In a small runway show, what five job assignments would probably be appointed (needed), besides the fashion show coordinator? _____

   _____

   _____

   _____

3. What are the uses for the fashion show coordinator's diary? _____

   _____

   _____

   _____

4. How might a fashion show audience be created? _____

   _____

   _____

   _____

5. If a designer/manufacturer, fashion magazine, or other organization is featured in a fashion show, what might be gained by including that sponsor in the theme? _____

   _____

   _____

   _____

(Continued)

Name_____

6. Name the major considerations when setting the date and time for a fashion show. _____

_____

_____

_____

7. With what factors is the location of the fashion show coordinated? _____

_____

_____

_____

8. What details should be checked before the date and place are booked for a fashion show?

_____

_____

_____

9. What types of details are included in a written contract for the site of a fashion show? _____

_____

_____

_____

10. What types of written documents can help to prevent losses and legal problems during and after
    the show? _____

_____

_____

11. Name at least three ways that audience safety can be provided during fashion shows. _____

_____

_____

_____

12. How do retailers usually recover the costs of producing a fashion show? _____

_____

_____

_____

13. When space is rented for a fashion show, what factors affect the price? _____

_____

_____

_____

Fashion Event Fill-in-the-Blanks

Activity B   **Name** _____

Chapter 23   **Date** _____ **Period**_____

Complete each of the following sentences by filling in the blanks.

1. A _____ is a spoken explanation of what is going on in a fashion show, especially pointing out specific features of each outfit being modeled.

2. Trying on merchandise by models ahead of a fashion show to see how the garments look and fit are called _____.

3. A draft of a print advertisement is a _____.

4. _____ _____ are promotional activities held to build customer traffic, sell goods, and enhance a company's image.

5. _____ _____ are theatrical presentations of apparel, accessories, and other fashion products on live models to audiences.

6. _____ are people who help fashion show models change and care for the clothes.

7. A _____ audience for a fashion show is established after the show is planned, as a result of publicity and advertising.

8. Elevated fashion show walkways for models that project out from the stage, usually into the audience seating area, are _____.

9. _____ is the planned arrangement of movement, such as with specific dance steps or gestured moves in a fashion show.

10. The order in which outfits will appear in a fashion show is called the _____.

11. _____ are turns made by models in fashion shows, most often at the halfway point and end of the runway.

12. Physically disassembling the set of a fashion show and returning props and equipment is known as _____ _____ _____.

13. A _____ _____ arrangement has rows of chairs lined up side-by-side, facing a stage or fashion show runway.

14. The most elaborate and expensive type of fashion show, with entertainment, backdrops, and lighting effects, is referred to as a _____ _____.

15. Jointly sponsored fashion shows, with expenses shared by two or more organizations, are called _____ fashion shows.

16. The combination of different music selections to create specific moods, for instance for a fashion show, is called the _____ _____.

17. A _____ _____ is a private fashion showing for the press before the public sees the fashions.

18. _____ modeling presents fashions informally by walking from table to table in a restaurant, to show-and-tell about what is being worn.

19. Fashion show seating, often at round tables, when a meal is served in conjunction with the show is called _____ _____.

(Continued)

Name_____

20. A _____ _____ _____ is a typical fashion show presentation with models parading on a runway in a certain order of appearance.

21. People who cue fashion show models onto the stage in the correct order and at the right time, guided by the lineup and commentary script, are called _____.

22. The _____ _____ for a fashion show is the removing of items to be modeled from the sales floor to a show storage area.

23. An _____ fashion show is a casual presentation of garments and accessories, without a runway or commentary.

24. A _____ audience for a fashion show is established before the show is organized and will attend regardless of the show.

25. The practice sessions for fashion shows are called _____.

26. The person in charge of an entire fashion show presentation is the fashion show _____.

27. An advertisement torn directly from the newspaper in which it ran is called a _____ _____.

28. A fashion show planning device that names all merchandise categories to be presented and the number of garments to be selected per category is an _____ _____.

29. Fashion shows presented by retailers to consumers are called _____ fashion shows.

30. The _____ _____ includes all the models that will be in a fashion show, including names, telephone numbers, and apparel sizes.

31. The first step in planning a fashion show budget is to forecast expected _____ (incomes) for the show.

32. The fashion show budget should include an _____ _____ as a "cushion" that covers unexpected costs or overruns of expenses.

Setting the Groundwork

Activity C   Name _____

Chapter 23   Date _____ Period_____

A fashion show might be staged to raise money for charity, to train salespeople about a store's new merchandise, or to stimulate customers to buy certain merchandise. Whatever the purpose for the show, similar duties must be accomplished and the same basic written forms should be used to record and organize needed information.

With the class divided into six groups of students, develop the forms for a fashion show that were not given in the book chapter. Each group should complete a different form. All students should review the section of the chapter that pertains to their form, and do further research if required. The "generic" forms that should be drawn up will have labeled spaces for the type of information needed, but will not include any specific details.

The following forms should be developed:

1. An ideal chart.

2. A confirmation sheet for booking models to be in the show.

3. A model list form for the show.

4. A lineup form for outfits and models.

5. A commentary card form.

6. An evaluation form to use after the show has been presented.

The form I am developing is #_____ in the above list.

Names of others in my group: _____

_____

_____

_____

Background material in the textbook is on pages: _____

Additional available reference material: _____

_____

_____

Information categories needed on the form include: _____

_____

_____

_____

_____

Produce a Fashion Show

Activity D   **Name** _____

Chapter 23   **Date** _____ **Period**_____

The best way to learn is by doing! With the entire class involved, produce a fashion show that features fashions sewn by students or clothes from cooperating retail stores. Appoint people for the jobs that need to be done, as well as the modeling. Prepare all of the necessary forms as described in the text. Prepare a schedule for the timing of promotion, fittings, set construction, rehearsals, etc. Assign jobs such as choreography and model training, invitations/tickets/programs, set design, music, refreshments, and other necessary duties to the appropriate chairpeople. Also, make sure that safety and security precautions are taken. (Attach all forms and notes to this page.)

The fashion show coordinator will be _____

The theme of the show will be _____

The audience will consist of _____

Committee chairpeople are: _____

    Merchandise coordinator: _____

    Model coordinator: _____

    Stage manager: _____

    Promotion coordinator: _____

    Commentator: _____

    Hospitality coordinator: _____

    Other: _____

    _____

The time and place for the show will be: _____

_____

My responsibilities for the show: _____

Schedule for what I must accomplish: _____

_____

_____

_____

_____

_____

_____

_____

A Global

Perspective

Global Review

Activity A   **Name** _____

Chapter 24   **Date** _____ **Period**_____

Respond to the following about global trade.

1. What country provides the largest amount of imported textile and apparel items for U.S. consumers? _____

_____

_____

2. What does trade involve? _____

_____

_____

3. Why must the U.S. government be careful about restricting imports of fashion merchandise from certain countries? _____

_____

_____

4. What U.S. government committee negotiates and administers individual textile/apparel agreements and quota programs? _____

_____

_____

5. Name two areas of the world today that are in the agricultural stage of development. _____

_____

_____

6. In general, do developed and developing countries import or export more goods respectively?

_____

_____

7. What is the name of the family or European countries united for free trade? _____

_____

_____

(Continued)

Name _____

8. What do CMT operations do? _____

_____

_____

9. Since NAFTA has been in effect, what has happened with imports and exports to and from Canada and Mexico? _____

_____

_____

10. Describe Mexico's workforce. _____

_____

_____

11. Why have retailers always favored free trade? _____

_____

_____

12. Through what cities do many imports come into the U.S. from Asia-Pacific and Latin America, respectively? _____

_____

_____

13. Describe an import merchant. _____

_____

_____

14. What is a wholly-owned subsidiary? _____

_____

_____

15. What two factors have made direct investment in the U.S. attractive to Asian and European firms?

_____

_____

_____

16. Although established markets are easier to enter than emerging markets, what problem might exist for businesses wanting to start in established markets? _____

_____

_____

17. What does international retailing (cross-border retailing) involve? _____

_____

_____

Global Differences

Activity B   **Name** _____

Chapter 24   **Date** _____ **Period** _____

In relation to this chapter, what is the difference between:

1. Import penetration and balance of trade? _____

   _____

   _____

   _____

   _____

2. Trade deficit and trade surplus? _____

   _____

   _____

   _____

   _____

3. Free trade and protectionism? _____

   _____

   _____

   _____

   _____

4. Market disruption and comparative advantage? _____

   _____

   _____

   _____

   _____

5. Transshipping and dumping? _____

   _____

   _____

   _____

   _____

6. Parity and value added? _____

   _____

   _____

   _____

   _____

(Continued)

Name_____

7. Structural adjustment and infrastructure? _____

_____

_____

_____

_____

8. Political stability and economic climate? _____

_____

_____

_____

_____

9. World Trade Organization (WTO) and North American Free Trade Agreement (NAFTA)? _____

_____

_____

_____

_____

10. Full package production and joint venture? _____

_____

_____

_____

_____

11. Globalization and multinational corporations (MNCs)? _____

_____

_____

_____

_____

12. Export merchants and export sales representatives? _____

_____

_____

_____

_____

Analyzing a Fashion Trade Article

Activity C   **Name** _____

Chapter 24   **Date** _____ **Period** _____

Obtain a news article from a current general or trade publication (newspaper or magazine) or from the Internet that deals with global aspects of fashion trade. Then cut out the article, mount it here, and analyze it according to the following questions.

1. What subject is being discussed? _____

   _____

   _____

2. Does the author seem to know the subject well? Why do you think so? _____

   _____

   _____

   _____

   _____

   _____

   _____

(Continued)

Name_____

3. Does the subject seem to be presented with a balanced point of view or is it slanted? Explain.

_____

_____

_____

_____

_____

4. How differently do you think you have interpreted the information in the news article after studying the chapter than you would have before learning the chapter content? _____

_____

_____

_____

_____

_____

5. What did you learn from this news article that you did not already know? _____

_____

_____

_____

_____

_____

6. Based upon information in this article, what future changes in international trade of textile/apparel products might you predict? _____

_____

_____

_____

_____

_____

Discussing Global Trade

Activity D   **Name** _____

Chapter 24   **Date** _____ **Period** _____

Read each of the following. On the lines provided, write down notes that you can use to contribute to a discussion of the information. Then, in small groups, or as a whole class, discuss the following information:

1. In China, Bangladesh, and other low-wage countries, "garment cities" have been built that have factories, shipping facilities, and worker housing to specialize in textile and apparel production. These "industrial campuses" are often near seaports for easy exporting of the goods that are made there.

   _____

   _____

2. Pure free trade assumes there is "perfect competition" in world markets, and that each nation produces goods for which it is most competitive.

   _____

   _____

3. Since many U.S. consumers do not care where goods are made, retail challenges of global sourcing include product development, quality, design, and speed-to-market besides cost.

   _____

   _____

4. Some foreign governments prefer to have only one or two major companies in industries where economies of scale provide a distinct advantage. They support and subsidize those companies, and argue that the larger firms have a better chance of competing in the world market. American producers up against this type of competition from abroad can make a very convincing case for U.S. government protection.

   _____

   _____

5. Sometimes countries _barter_, or exchange similar values of goods rather than using currency.

   _____

   _____

6. The U.S. has become mainly a service economy, since services (rather than manufacturing) account for most of the GDP and international trade.

   _____

   _____

7. Sometimes bilateral and multilateral agreements are signed to regulate trade between nations outside the WTO. _Bilateral agreements_ are between two countries, while _multilateral agreements_ are established among a group of several nations.

   _____

   _____

(Continued)

Name_____

8. As countries reach full development, large trade surpluses build up, enabling these countries to buy commodities and invest in other countries with their foreign exchange earnings. _Foreign exchange earnings_ are the invoice amounts or credits that the countries accumulate from selling their products to other countries.

_____

_____

9. The standard method of paying for merchandise ordered from overseas is with a letter of credit (LC). _A letter of credit_ is a document issued by a bank, guaranteeing payment of a customer's drafts up to a stated amount for a specified period. The bank's credit substitutes for the buyer's credit, and the LC describes the terms and conditions for payment. This eliminates the vendor's risk of not being paid after making and delivering the merchandise. However, it ties up the buyer's money, held by the bank, which could be spent for other goods during that time. The bank is paid a percentage of the value of the LC as a fee for performing the service.

_____

_____

10. China has geared up for vast manufacturing growth. Its textile/apparel industry originally bought used machinery from industrialized nations to get started. Now it has newer equipment. It is considered to be a threat to the textile and apparel industries of more developed countries.

_____

_____

11. Other Asian nations that are experiencing economic growth are India, Indonesia, Thailand, Sri Lanka, Malaysia, and the Philippines. Their textile and apparel industries are starting to be _foreign currency earners._

_____

_____

12. _Luxury products_, which are fashionable high-priced items retailed to wealthy consumers, are often sourced from Western European designers. France leads in luxury products, followed by Italy, Germany, and Great Britain. On the other hand, there have been large increases in low-priced imports from Eastern European countries (former Soviet Republics). Factories that used to supply fabric and apparel to the Soviet military are now making wool coats for the U.S. market.

_____

_____

13. When sourcing from abroad, sometimes a _freight-forwarding agent_ is used, who handles shipping details in offshore production from foreign countries.

_____

_____

(Continued)

Name_____

14. Many countries now have foreign trade offices that help companies interested in doing business within their borders. Of course, its information is heavily biased in favor of that country! The U.S. government also offers services such as political and credit-risk analysis, advice on market-entry strategy, and tips on sources of financing in various foreign countries. It introduces American firms to foreign business and government contacts and to potential importers, buyers, and agents.

_____

_____

15. Before opening businesses in other countries, U.S. companies should discover such things as trade trends, international agreements, and the size of the market in the company's niche in other parts of the world. U.S. companies should assess the political stability, extent of Westernization, and effect of local regulations on proposed ventures abroad.

_____

_____

16. To start exporting to overseas markets, reports are published by U.S. trade organizations and the government, such as _A Basic Guide to Exporting_. The Global Business Access organization in Washington, DC has a staff of retired ambassadors and foreign service experts who can be hired to evaluate overseas markets and cut through red tape. There are also "market access" guidebooks that have maps, economic data, and trade and investment opportunities. Additionally, Internet research can provide current, country-specific data on economics, culture, regulations, and government.

_____

_____

17. Small companies and those with little experience in international business might work through an agent with connections in the target country. _Export trading companies_ (ETCs) are intermediaries between U.S. exporters and foreign buyers. They are usually used by small- and medium-sized manufacturing firms. An _export cooperative_ is an export trading company formed and operated by several firms. By joining together, the firms in the cooperative gain economies of scale, price setting cooperation, financing advantages, and export knowledge.

_____

_____

18. The American Apparel Producers' Network runs a sourcing service of the Americas, offering every step in apparel production "from the dirt to the shirt!" Members carry out fiber/fabric/trim sourcing, domestic and offshore design/cutting/sewing, shipping issues, replenishment, and both CMT and full package production. They even have an online sourcing database.

_____

_____

Researching Global Fashion

Activity E   **Name** _____

Chapter 24   **Date** _____   **Period** _____

With a small group, pick one of the following activities. When completed, present your material to the rest of the class. Following your presentation, allow other classmates to ask questions, add to the discussion, or give constructive criticism.

A.   Research the International Apparel Sourcing Show, Hispanic Retail 360, or the World Retail Congress by doing library and Internet research. You may also research another international textile/apparel show or meeting that interests you. Find out when and where the event takes place, who sponsors it, what types of companies or countries are exhibitors, who attends, what trade groups endorse it, what types of educational seminars are offered, and other interesting information.

B.   Research an international textile/apparel magazine, such as *Mundo Textil*. Describe the types of information it includes, who its readers are, who advertises in the magazine, how large the circulation is, etc. Obtain copies of the magazine, if possible, to study and show.

C.   Research a U.S. trade law, such as the Trade and Tariff Act, Customs Modernization and Informed Compliance Act, Foreign Trade Antitrust Improvements Act, Export Company Trading Company Act, or others that you find to be interesting. Find out when the law was passed, how it affects U.S. textile/apparel trade, its strong and weak points for jobs and other aspects of our economy, what trade groups or industry sectors were for or against its passage, and other pertinent information.

D.   Research a U.S. trade pact or agreement that involves other countries, such as NAFTA, DR-CAFTA, General Agreement on Tariffs and Trade (GATT), Trade and Development Act of 2000 (TDA), etc. How was it organized or drawn up, what is its content, what does textile/apparel trade literature say for or against it, and what might it lead to for the future of U.S. fashion businesses and trade?

E.   Research an emerging market for textile/apparel products, so you can analyze it for possible U.S. fashion exporting. Indicate how big its market is (population numbers by sex, age, etc.), what the buying power is (the standard of living or amount of disposable income), how fast its economy is growing, societal trends that affect fashion purchases, currency exchange, laws or trade agreements about importing or selling fashion goods from other countries, cities or other locations that would have the highest demand for fashion goods, its domestic supply of fashion goods, what types of retailers or other fashion businesses are in existence (competition), etc.

Letter of the activity chosen: _____

Names of those in the group and their assignments for this project:

_____

_____

_____

Attach your research notes to this page.

The Latest Fashion Business Trends

Business Trends Quiz

Activity A

Chapter 25

Name _____

Date _____ Period_____

Write one true/false question for each of the chapter sections noted, and write the correct answers on another piece of paper. If your question is false, write the sentence correctly (true) on your other piece of paper. Then exchange workbook pages with a classmate to try to answer each other's questions correctly on this page. Check answers with the prepared answer sheet.

True or False

Satisfying a Changing Consumer Market:

_____ 1. _____

_____

_____

The Importance of Demographics and Psychographics:

_____ 2. _____

_____

_____

Niche Marketing:

_____ 3. _____

_____

_____

Database Research for Niche Marketing:

_____ 4. _____

_____

_____

(Continued)

Name_____

Trends in Retail Formats—Discount Retailing:

_____ 5.   _____

_____

_____

Nonstore Retailing:

_____ 6.   _____

_____

_____

Direct-Mail Marketing:

_____ 7.   _____

_____

_____

TV Home Shopping Sales:

_____ 8.   _____

_____

_____

Online Retailing:

_____ 9.   _____

_____

_____

Omni-Channel Retailing:

_____10.   _____

_____

_____

Strategy and Technology Review

Activity B   **Name** _____

Chapter 25   **Date** _____ **Period**_____

Answer the following questions about the latest textile/apparel business strategy and technology.

1. The tougher fashion business climate is a result of what two main conditions? _____

   _____

   _____

   _____

2. How is horizontal consolidation of the industry being accomplished? _____

   _____

   _____

   _____

3. For retailers to expand, what is easier and less expensive than building new stores? _____

   _____

   _____

   _____

4. What is the meaning of divestiture? _____

   _____

   _____

   _____

5. What is a takeover? _____

   _____

   _____

   _____

6. Why are companies that successfully resist takeover bids often left in poorer financial condition?

   _____

   _____

   _____

7. How do retailers try to downsize with no loss in volume? _____

   _____

   _____

   _____

(Continued)

Name _____

8. What is the objective of Chapter 11 bankruptcies? _____

_____

_____

_____

9. What percentage of the total owed to them by a Chapter 7 bankrupt business would parties receive
    if liquidation resulted in a settlement of outstanding debts of fifty cents on the dollar? _____

_____

_____

_____

10. Consolidation of retailers has resulted in what type of concentration? _____

_____

_____

_____

11. Why have private label goods become more accepted by consumers? _____

_____

_____

_____

12. For the fashion industry, what does supply chain collaboration mean? _____

_____

_____

_____

13. In the future, from what kind (color) of fabric will garments be cut, to avoid excess inventories of
    many different patterned materials? _____

_____

_____

_____

14. What do we mean when we say that retail stores may become storefronts in the future?

_____

_____

_____

15. In the future, how will the lead times for garment manufacturing be different from today? _____

_____

_____

_____

Fashion Business Trends Fill-in-the-Blanks

Activity C   Name _____

Chapter 25   Date _____ Period _____

Complete the following statements by filling in the blanks.

1. The purchase of another company, with the buying company gaining the controlling interest, is called a(n) _____.

2. Large-scale, long-range planning for achieving an organization's objectives is called _____.

3. Online _____ is the selling of merchandise to consumers through personal computers and smartphones.

4. Buying _____ is power in the marketplace that enables companies who have it to get promotions, rebates, and additional discounts from suppliers.

5. _____ (CPFR) is a management concept that is enabled by data synchronization technology used over the Internet.

6. _____ is customer analysis that uses software to discover patterns within a data warehouse and derive actionable responses.

7. Small lots of new designs brought to market quickly through supply chain collaboration is called _____.

8. _____ management is a retail strategy of managing product groups as business units and customizing them on a store-by-store basis to better satisfy customer needs.

9. _____ performance is the individual quality of work done by each employee and the overall performance of the department or company as a whole.

10. Power _____ are shopping areas with several large discount retailers on the same site, and usually in close proximity to a regional mall.

11. Consumer-_____ retailing is nonstore selling to consumers who shop from home.

12. _____ TV is two-way television selling that consists of graphic and written presentations of merchandise that is shown and can be ordered through the technology.

13. _____ is the dividing of an industry's total market into extremely narrowly defined target markets.

14. Niche _____ is a specialty viewpoint in which departments or stores identify and closely target specific fashion tastes.

15. _____ retailers operate a seamless combination of stores, catalogs, websites, and sometimes TV channels.

16. Body _____ is a procedure to collect individual sizing information electronically.

17. The inability to pay debts is called _____.

18. Mass _____ is offering individually-made items to everyone.

(Continued)

Name _____

19. The preference of people to stay at home is called _____.

20. _____-backs are penalties or claims against vendors for not following the many different rules set by each retailer.

21. Restructuring by uniting of two or more parts into one is called _____.

22. The existence of too many stores and shopping centers in a retail trading area, all vying for limited consumer dollars is called _____.

23. _____-shopping is the consumer trend of combining purchases from both ends of the price scale.

24. When a company _____, it sells off all assets and uses the proceeds to pay outstanding debts on a percentage basis.

25. Niche _____ is the production of specific lines of goods for carefully defined customers.

26. _____ manufacturing is a "seamless" data capture system of production and delivery that makes information-based decisions quickly.

27. _____ retailing is the showing of consumer's own images on the screen to see how specific clothing will look on them.

28. The joining of two companies to form a new one is called a _____.

29. Electronic _____ are computer-simulated stores that consumers can scroll through by aisle, product category, or item.

30. The reduction of the size of a business to reduce costs and become more efficient is called _____.

31. A television home sales technique that is heavy on information, to educate and build intimacy with customers is called _____.

32. _____ involves examining a business to see what changes can make it better, reallocating resources and employees, and recharting its course.

33. _____ (B2C) commerce is the electronic selling of goods by companies to shoppers.

Business Trends Know-How

Activity D	**Name** _____
Chapter 25	**Date** _____ **Period**_____

Write your thoughts about the following statements on the lines, and try to expand the topic further. Then share your thoughts with others by having a class discussion about each statement.

1. There is a glut of similarly-stocked stores because of the industry's risk aversion. This encourages conservative strategies that try to minimize downside losses in the intensely competitive environment. More risk-taking is needed, leaning toward opportunistic strategies where bold moves can produce big long-term payoffs from innovative offensiveness.

   _____

   _____

   _____

   _____

2. Since outstanding customer service is fundamental to fashion industry success, effective employee training can develop a "culture" of good service through competent salespeople.

   _____

   _____

   _____

   _____

3. Retailers must stop blaming poor sales volumes on bad weather, unpopular apparel designs, or the apathy of consumers. They must take action to create higher sales volumes.

   _____

   _____

   _____

   _____

4. Yes, the U.S. is overstored. In the early 1990s, there were over 18 square feet of retail space for every man, woman, and child in the U.S., and more space has been added since then.

   _____

   _____

   _____

   _____

5. The goal of shoppers is to purchase the best products for the best prices in smooth, convenient ways. This can be done today via "retail without boundaries!"

   _____

   _____

   _____

   _____

(Continued)

Name _____

6. Smart retail companies are seeking their own brand-name recognition and reliable sources of supply. Being responsive with private label efforts and marketing skills can satisfy customers, add prestige to the store, and increase margins.

_____

_____

_____

_____

7. We are approaching the end of the retail world as we have known it. There will be more change in the next three years than in any period of the last 100 years!

_____

_____

_____

_____

8. Internet access each year has doubled since 1980, with global websites available to all people with Internet access. U.S. consumers can buy from companies in other parts of the world, and vice versa.

_____

_____

_____

_____

9. Companies are no longer built to last—now they are built to change. They are no longer responsible for the customer—they must now be responsive to the customer.

_____

_____

_____

_____

_____

_____

_____

10. Mergers and acquisitions, over time, change the industry structure and relative positions of the participants. However, companies can't just gain strength and market share by buying others; they must also respond to market needs or they will have a large white elephant!

_____

_____

_____

Alphabet Soup

Activity E   **Name** _____

Chapter 25   **Date** _____ **Period** _____

Write the letter of the correct word from the list at the right on the line of the matching description on the left. Then answer the following questions.

_____ 1. **A** reorganizes to become A.

_____ 2. B and C join to become BC.

_____ 3. D sells its assets to no longer exist.

_____ 4. E gets controlling interest of F and becomes **E**F.

_____ 5. **G** streamlines to become G.

_____ 6. H buys I and becomes H.

_____ 7. **JK** sells half of its organization and becomes J.

A. acquisition
B. Chapter 7 bankruptcy
C. Chapter 11 bankruptcy
D. divestiture
E. downsizing
F. merger
G. takeover

8. The "LMN Manufacturing Company" has been doing large volume manufacturing, taking advantage of economies of scale. Then it pushes the product to sell in the market. It has a good research and development laboratory that constantly tries to improve the company's product line. What changes should the company probably make to be successful in the future?

_____

_____

_____

9. The "OPQ Retail Company" is afraid to make changes in its store format and management style because it has been quite successful during previous decades. It has many layers of management through which employees can be "groomed" as they work their way toward the top. This also creates nice control of the job activities of employees. How might this company change to be successful in the future?

_____

_____

_____

10. "RST Fashions" makes and sells basic women's shorts, skirts, and tops. It has expanded with manufacturing plants in several states and factory outlet stores throughout the U.S. Merchandise that doesn't sell is priced low and sent to the company's one store in Mexico. What changes might RST Fashions consider for success in the future?

_____

_____

_____

Is a Fashion Career in Your Future?

Fashion Career Planning Maze

Activity A

Chapter 26

Name _____

Date _____ **Period** _____

Draw a line through this maze from "start" to "great career." Have your line cross 10 phrases that apply to successful fashion career planning. When you finish the maze, write the 10 phrases in the order they appear in the maze, to create a list that reviews the fashion career planning process. Then make a list of the wrong ways to plan a fashion career, in any order, that your line did not cross.

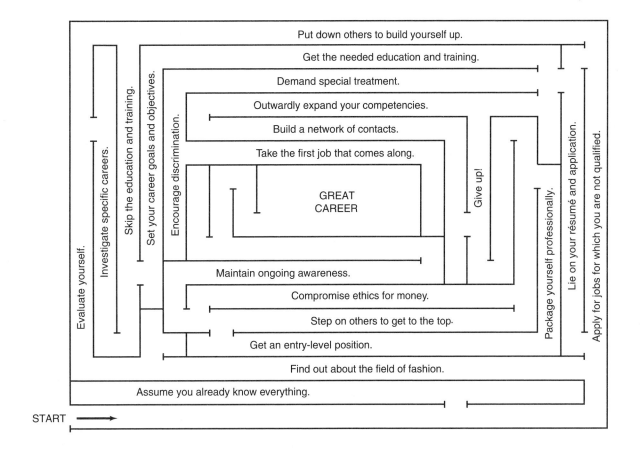

Maze phrases:

Put down others to build yourself up.
Get the needed education and training.
Demand special treatment.
Outwardly expand your competencies.
Build a network of contacts.
Take the first job that comes along.

GREAT CAREER

Evaluate yourself.
Investigate specific careers.
Skip the education and training.
Set your career goals and objectives.
Encourage discrimination.
Give up!
Package yourself professionally.
Lie on your résumé and application.
Apply for jobs for which you are not qualified.

Maintain ongoing awareness.
Compromise ethics for money.
Step on others to get to the top.
Get an entry-level position.
Find out about the field of fashion.
Assume you already know everything.

START ⟶

(Continued)

Name _____

Successful fashion career planning

1. _____
2. _____
3. _____
4. _____
5. _____
6. _____
7. _____
8. _____
9. _____
10. _____

Poor fashion career planning

1. _____
2. _____
3. _____
4. _____
5. _____
6. _____
7. _____
8. _____
9. _____
10. _____
11. _____

A Career Self-Evaluation

Activity B   **Name** _____

Chapter 26   **Date** _____ **Period** _____

A. Complete a career self-evaluation by writing serious answers to these questions. This will not be seen by others, except your teacher when you turn it in as a completed assignment.

1. What are my likes and dislikes? _____

   _____

   _____

2. Do I like to work alone, with a few coworkers, or with the general public? _____

   _____

   _____

3. Do I like to travel or work at the same place every day? _____

   _____

   _____

4. Would I prefer to live where I live now, or in a large city, small town, or foreign country? _____

   _____

   _____

5. Would I like to work regular weekday hours or be willing to work on weekends and holidays with assorted days off during the middle of the week? _____

   _____

   _____

6. Do I like to perform scientific experiments doing research? _____

   _____

   _____

7. Do I like the creativity of sewing, drawing, or writing? _____

   _____

   _____

8. Do my interests seem to revolve around products, people, or data? _____

   _____

   _____

9. Am I more comfortable following or leading others? _____

   _____

   _____

10. Am I a good organizer or do I like to do work that is organized by others? _____

    _____

    _____

(Continued)

Name_____

11. Do I prefer repeated activities such as factory work? _____
_____
_____

12. Do I like to make decisions such as deciding about managerial strategy? _____
_____
_____

13. Do I enjoy a variety of changing activities such as sales or administrative work? _____
_____
_____

14. Do I prefer physical activity or desk work? _____
_____
_____

15. Do I like calm times or do I handle challenges and pressure well? _____
_____
_____

16. How important to me are money, prestige, or security? _____
_____
_____

17. Might I work better in a large or small company/organization? _____
_____
_____

18. What are my employment-related strengths and weaknesses? _____
_____
_____

B. Now look at the chart in Illustration 26-8 of the text. Write your top three choices from the chart and evaluate how they relate to your answers in Part A of this activity.

1. _____   _____
_____   _____
_____   _____

2. _____   _____
_____   _____
_____   _____

3. _____   _____
_____   _____
_____   _____

Fashion Careers Terms Match

Activity C   **Name** _____

Chapter 26   **Date** _____ **Period**_____

Match the following terms and definitions by placing the correct letter(s) next to each number. (Complete the first and second lists separately.)

_____ 1. A college degree earned at the completion of most four-year programs.

_____ 2. A lifelong field of employment, or vocation, through which people progress.

_____ 3. A person's abilities of doing specific tasks.

_____ 4. A person's talents, or what the person is naturally good at doing.

_____ 5. A specific field of study in college.

_____ 6. A specific work assignment or position within an industry, with certain duties, roles, or functions.

_____ 7. A team approach between employees and educational institutions that gives students on-the-job training for future careers.

_____ 8. A written statement of what the employee holding a specific job is expected to do.

_____ 9. An educational degree earned with most community college programs, usually of two years in length.

_____ 10. Beginning jobs in a career.

_____ 11. Clubs and sports outside of school classes.

_____ 12. Curriculums completed in trade schools.

_____ 13. High school educational programs in which students learn the skills for entry-level employment.

_____ 14. Exchange programs with schools in other parts of the country or world.

_____ 15. Executive trainee programs for college graduates to become future managers with a company.

_____ 16. High-level jobs held by strategic thinkers who are devoted employees.

_____ 17. Jobs concerned with running a business.

_____ 18. Jobs that involve a higher degree of responsibility than lower management jobs.

_____ 19. Overall term for the tasks and employees concerned with running a company.

A. administration
B. apprenticeship
C. aptitudes
D. associate's degree
E. bachelor's degree
F. career
G. career path
H. career planning
I. certificate courses
J. college major
K. cooperative (co-op) programs
L. entry-level jobs
M. extracurricular activities
N. internships
O. job
P. job description
Q. job security
R. management positions
S. management training programs
T. middle management
U. reciprocal agreements
V. skills
W. upper management
X. vocational/career programs
Y. work-study programs

(Continued)

Name _____

_____ 20. The order of jobs worked in a person's life.

_____ 21. The process of laying out employees' futures with a firm based on the firm's needs and each employee's strengths and weaknesses.

_____ 22. Training for an occupation by working under the direction and guidance of a skilled worker.

_____ 23. Work-study programs at the college level.

_____ 24. Work-study programs at the high school and trade school levels of education.

_____ 25. Assurance of keeping one's employment.

(Continued)

Name_____

_____ 1. A written statement that sets forth the legal principles that should guide that organization's decisions.

_____ 2. A predetermined pay rate per hour spent doing a job.

_____ 3. The lowest hourly rate established by law.

_____ 4. A U.S. law making it illegal to discriminate against people with disabilities.

_____ 5. A fixed amount of pay, usually received once or twice a month, for doing all that is required for a particular job.

_____ 6. Total of wages, salary, and benefits given for work done.

_____ 7. The use of good moral values in business dealings.

_____ 8. Extra pay awarded at the end of the year, based on the company's profits for the year and length of time a worker has been with the company.

_____ 9. Employment rewards in addition to wages or salary.

_____ 10. Payments and benefits for work accomplished.

_____ 11. The treating of people differently, related to prejudice rather than work performance.

_____ 12. The length of time an employee has been in a job compared to others who do the same job.

_____ 13. Extra monetary payment in addition to regular pay.

_____ 14. Certain amounts of money subtracted from paychecks, such as for taxes and Social Security.

_____ 15. Extra niceties for employees with high stature in the company.

_____ 16. Extra pay that rewards high sales or productivity during a certain period of time.

_____ 17. A written document that deals with employee standards and "corporate culture-building."

_____ 18. Time worked beyond the usual 40-hour week.

_____ 19. Money or a gift accepted by a trusted employee from an outsider trying to influence the employee's judgment or conduct.

_____ 20. The blending of different races, cultures, genders, ages, socioeconomic backgrounds, personality types, and intelligence levels into a productive employment team.

_____ 21. When business decisions influence personal gain.

_____ 22. Events where companies and job applicants attend, to connect with each other.

AA.   Americans with Disabilities Act
BB.   bonus
CC.   bribe
DD.   business ethics
EE.   career fairs
FF.   code of ethics
GG.   compensation
HH.   compensation package
II.   conflicts of interest
JJ.   deductions
KK.   employment discrimination
LL.   fringe benefits
MM.   hourly wage
NN.   incentive bonus
OO.   minimum wage
PP.   overtime
QQ.   perquisites or "perks"
RR.   salary
SS.   seniority
TT.   value statement
UU.   workplace diversity
VV.   year-end bonus

Research and Report

Activity D   **Name** _____

Chapter 26   **Date** _____ **Period**_____

With a group of classmates, select one of the following activities. After completing research about the subject, present your material to the rest of the class. When you are finished, allow classmates to ask questions or add comments.

A. Do research to find out about the Equal Employment Opportunity Commission (EEOC) and the laws the commission oversees.

B. Do research to find out about the Occupational Safety and Health Administration (OSHA) and the employment standards it oversees.

C. Do research to find out about the employment conditions that are regulated by the Fair Labor Standards Act.

D. Do research to find out about two actual work-study programs, one a cooperative program at the high school/trade school level and one an internship at the college level.

Letter of the activity chosen: _____

Names of those in the group and their assignments for this project:

_____

_____

_____

_____

_____

_____

My sources of information and notes about their content:

_____

_____

_____

_____

_____

_____

Textile and Apparel Careers

Categorizing Jobs

Activity A   Name _____

Chapter 27   Date _____ Period _____

Most jobs in textile and apparel companies can be placed within general types of work. Look at the following categories, represented by letters, and place the letter of the appropriate category on the line in front of each employee listed below. Keep in mind that distribution (not listed) is also an important category of textile/apparel business.

R = Research and development

D = Design

P = Production

S = Sales

_____	1. Fabric structural designer		_____	11. Fashion designer
_____	2. Textile laboratory technician		_____	12. Pattern grader
_____	3. Sketcher		_____	13. Traveling salesperson
_____	4. Production supervisor		_____	14. Textile tester
_____	5. Apparel marker/spreader		_____	15. Merchandise coordinator
_____	6. Showroom salesperson		_____	16. Plant engineer
_____	7. Quality control inspector		_____	17. Design stylist
_____	8. Finisher		_____	18. Presser
_____	9. Textile research scientist		_____	19. Sales trainee
_____	10. Print/repeat artist		_____	20. Sewing machine operator

After analyzing the answers, which of the general categories appeals the most to you and why?

_____

_____

_____

_____

(Continued)

Name _____

In the labor-intensive textile and apparel industries, what general category has the most employees? How is this changing for the future?

_____

_____

_____

_____

_____

_____

_____

_____

Textile / Apparel Employment Review

Activity B   **Name** _____

Chapter 27   **Date** _____ **Period** _____

As you review the chapter, respond to the following questions.

1. What advantages are there for graduate students who do research at universities? _____

   _____

   _____

2. Name three specific procedures that textile laboratory technicians perform, that may be repetitive
   and are learned on the job. _____

   _____

   _____

   _____

3. Why is textile design important to companies later in the soft goods chain? _____

   _____

   _____

4. Before computers were used to do structural fabric designs, how were the designs created?

   _____

   _____

5. Name four types of organizations that employ fabric surface designers. _____

   _____

   _____

   _____

   _____

6. What is the difference between the jobs of assistant to the stylist and assistant stylist? _____

   _____

   _____

7. What is another name for the fashion director position? _____

   _____

   _____

8. To whom do fashion directors send fabric presentations? _____

   _____

   _____

9. In what physical format do fabric libraries keep information about their fibers and fabrics?

   _____

   _____

(Continued)

Name_____

10. What do textile production workers do? _____

_____

_____

11. What do plant engineers do? _____

_____

12. The greatest number of apparel design employees work for manufacturers of what level of goods?

_____

_____

13. In what kind of firms do most opportunities for assistant fashion designers exist? _____

_____

_____

14. Why must fashion designers have patience? _____

_____

_____

15. What does a sample maker do? _____

_____

_____

16. What type of apparel producer would most likely employ finishers? _____

_____

_____

17. What does a marketing manager do? _____

_____

_____

18. To whom do fiber salespeople and greige goods producers sell their goods? _____

_____

_____

19. How are salespeople often paid? _____

_____

_____

20. Define showroom salespeople. _____

_____

_____

Careers Fill-in-the-Blanks

Activity C   **Name** _____

Chapter 27   **Date** _____ **Period** _____

Place the correct chapter term into each of the following sentences. All terms asked for are in **bold** print or *italics* in the textbook chapter.

1. Apparel company employees who do freehand drawings of ideas that designers have draped onto mannequins in fabric are called _____.

2. _____ _____ are supervisors of several sales representatives in an established "district" of the country or a division of the company.

3. The job title for an executive who determines the fashion direction the business will take, and communicates that information throughout the organization is _____ _____.

4. A _____ _____ is a fabric designer who does original textile surface designs of motifs, color combinations, and repeats.

5. A design idea or theme, which usually repeats itself in a continuous pattern in fabric surface designs, is a _____.

6. _____ _____ are employees who manage distribution centers and try to get products quickly from manufacturing facilities to customers.

7. _____ _____ are apparel company employees who cut out and sew design samples.

8. A _____ that includes loose, unfolded art or design papers showing a person's creative work is often required when that person seeks artistic or design jobs.

9. A _____ _____ is in charge of a manufactured fiber company's fabric library.

10. Manufacturing executives who are in charge of every aspect of one of the company's lines or a specific category of items within a line are _____ _____.

11. _____ _____ are cost and efficiency experts who save companies time and money.

12. _____ _____ are manufacturing employees who make sure all environmental systems are operating properly.

13. Textile company employees who interpret fashion into new woven or knitted patterns are _____ _____ _____.

14. _____ _____ are manufacturing company employees who coordinate and direct various manufacturing operations.

15. Employees who create ideas that combine function and beauty into new garments are _____ _____.

16. _____ _____ are apparel production employees who correct production defects.

17. A _____ _____ is a textile employee who arranges prints on fabrics after the motifs and colors have been established.

(Continued)

Name _____

18. _____ _____ are employees who conduct market research to try to discover future market needs.

19. _____ _____ _____ work in all phases of production to analyze the quality of items being manufactured.

20. A _____ works out different color combinations for fabric surface designs.

21. _____ _____ _____ are purchasing agents who research and buy the fabrics, trims, and notions that are chosen by their apparel company designers and approved by management.

22. _____ _____ work for apparel companies as fashion design copyists.

23. _____ _____ work for textile firms coordinating fabric design, production, and sales between the creative and business aspects of the company.

24. The _____ _____ is the executive in charge of all operations and employees at a manufacturing plant.

25. A _____ _____ for a textile firm is an executive responsible for an entire type of merchandise or market category.

26. A manufacturing employee who determines the overall price of producing each item is a _____ _____.

27. _____ _____ are textile industry employees who test new products against required specifications or standards of quality.

28. Textile company employees who translate the company's color choices and applied print looks onto fabrics are called _____ _____ _____.

29. Manufacturing employees who cut patterns in all of the different sizes produced by the manufacturer are _____ _____.

30. _____ _____ _____ are textile industry employees who help conduct research, often working under research scientists.

Developing a Textile or Apparel Line

Activity D   Name _____

Chapter 27   Date _____   Period_____

With the class divided into two halves, one group of students should "become" the employees of the ABC Textile Company and the other half should form the XYZ Apparel Company. The students who are assigned to the following jobs should study more about those jobs by doing research and possibly communicating with people who actually work in the jobs. Some jobs may be combined (especially in apparel production) or divided if needed, so all students have a job assignment. The company should develop a sample line (with pictures, samples, or sketches). Then, in a presentation to the other half of the class, all "employees" should describe the specific tasks involved in doing their jobs, what preparation is required to get the job, and what they would do in a real working situation to accomplish the company's goals. Each company may also have a sales manager, to introduce to the audience the company's general type of merchandise, target market, image, the specific line, and/or other details.

ABC Textile Company

Job Title	Student Assigned to That Job
Textile research scientist	
Textile laboratory technician	
Textile tester	
Fabric structural designer	
Fabric surface designer (or print/repeat artist, colorist, and strike-off artist)	
Fabric stylist (plus assistant)	
Fashion director (plus assistant)	
Department manager	
Fabric librarian	
Market analyst	
Textile production workers	
Production supervisor	
Quality control inspector	
Plant engineer	
Industrial engineer	
Narrator (Sales manager)	

Ideas about the line to be developed: _____

_____

_____

(Continued)

Name_____

XYZ Apparel Company

Job Title	Student Assigned to That Job
Fashion designer, or design stylist; (plus assistant)	
Sketcher (plus assistant)	
Costing engineer (plus costing clerk)	
Piece goods buyer	
Sample cutter	
Sample maker	
Pattern maker	
Pattern grader	
Marker	
Spreader	
Cutter	
Assorter	
Sewing machine operators (what tasks)	
Finisher	
Inspector/trimmer	
Presser	
Production supervisor	
Plant manager (plus production assistant)	
Product manager	
Marketing manager	
Narrator (Sales manager)	

Ideas about the line to be developed: _____

_____

_____

_____

_____

_____

_____

Match the Qualifications

Activity E   Name _____

Chapter 27   Date _____ Period_____

Match each of the following job titles with the person whose qualifications meet it best.

_____ 1. Carlos has always had a flare for art. He is good at doing realistic, precise, and detailed drawings. His family is moving to a large city, and he is hoping to be able to find a job with an apparel manufacturing company.

_____ 2. Aidan enjoys the challenge of keeping the apparel production factory where he works operating smoothly. He maintains the facility's heating, lighting, noise reduction, and other environmental operations.

_____ 3. Emma is very smart and has an advanced degree in polymer chemistry. While attending college, she gained manufacturing experience in a textile plant through a work-study curriculum, but she prefers to work in a more controlled laboratory setting. She has just been hired by a fiber-producing company.

_____ 4. Julia is a new employee in the design department of a large firm that mass-produces lower-priced apparel. Most of her work involves adapting higher-priced designs to meet the price range of her firm's customers. After gaining experience, she hopes to move up to a more creative position with a higher-priced line.

_____ 5. Makalya was employed by a large fabric mill for many years. At different times she worked as a colorist, print/repeat artist, and strike-off artist. After improving her CAD skills and deciding to change companies, she has found a position in which she will do all of these things for a small textile converter.

_____ 6. Jacob has a high school diploma, but no education or training beyond that. He lives near some apparel manufacturing plants and is willing to learn on the job. At an employment interview, he said that he has good tolerance for standing, steam, heat, and noise.

_____ 7. Olivia has been a successful department manager of both terrycloth and corduroy fabric types for a large textile mill. However, because of a company consolidation and downsizing, she had to seek a new position elsewhere. She was thrilled when offered this management job near the top of a smaller company that makes and sells only velvet fabrics.

A. costing engineer
B. design stylist/copyist
C. fabric librarian
D. fabric stylist
E. fabric surface designer
F. finisher
G. management trainee
H. pattern maker
I. plant engineer
J. presser
K. production supervisor
L. sales manager
M. showroom manager
N. showroom salesperson
O. sketching assistant
P. textile research scientist
Q. traffic manager
R. vice president of merchandising

(Continued)

Name _____

_____ 8. Taylor has proven himself as a leader in extracurricular activities during high school and college. He is going into production management with an apparel manufacturing firm. His career will start in two weeks, after he gets his diploma in apparel production engineering.

_____ 9. Vince has worked hard at his sales rep job and has a long, successful record of achievement. With his experience and knowledge of the field, he is ready to take on more responsibility in the firm.

_____ 10. Maria lives near an exclusive wedding gown manufacturer that makes high-quality items by special order. Although she cannot sketch or make patterns, Maria is able to use the hand sewing skills taught to her by her grandmother in her work for the firm.

_____ 11. Tanya has worked for a firm as a costing clerk and assistant piece goods buyer. She is familiar with the prices of fabrics and notions used to produce the company's garments, as well as the production processes necessary to produce them. She is good with numbers, and a management job has recently opened up to which she has been assigned.

_____ 12. Ethan is good with computers and quantitative details. He worked in a distribution warehouse during the summers of his schooling years. Since graduating from college, he has been a transportation specialist with an apparel company. Now he has been promoted to manage the distribution center.

_____ 13. After being a top-notch showroom salesperson, Shanaya has recently been promoted. She enjoys her supervisory duties and makes sure that everything is prepared perfectly for buyers' visits to see the displayed apparel samples.

_____ 14. Lisa works for a manufactured fiber company. She maintains an up-to-date visual collection of fabrics made of the firm's fibers. She tries to show how the fibers and fabrics satisfy the latest trends of the fashion industry.

_____ 15. Hilario is an employee at the company's sales facility in Los Angeles. He shows visiting buyers the newest features and colors of his company's apparel lines. He feels a sense of pride when he writes up the orders, knowing that he has accomplished a sale.

_____ 16. Emily has a similar job with an apparel company as her friend, Eduardo, has with a textile mill. They graduated from engineering college together, and each went through the management training program of their respective companies. Emily oversees the sewing machine operators at the apparel firm, for the best work to be accomplished, while Eduardo tries to maintain the highest worker productivity and product quality at his textile mill.

(Continued)

Name_____

_____ 17. Hannah was accustomed to doing her work with heavy paper, but her apparel production company modernized. They gave her specialized computer training, so now she translates the ideas of the design staff by computer, into the precise pieces that are needed to produce the styles in fabric.

_____ 18. Trevon has worked hard for a textile company for many years, and has continued to gain knowledge about textiles, long-range planning, and the consumer market. He has also developed many industry contacts and resources. The dedication to his career has paid off, because he is now in a high level job in which he coordinates the fabric design, production, and sales of the company's fabric lines.

Retail
Careers

Retail Employment Differences

Activity A **Name** _____

Chapter 28 **Date** _____ **Period** _____

In relation to this chapter, what is the difference between:

1. Two-functional organization and three-functional organization? _____

_____

_____

_____

_____

_____

2. Departmental buyer and classification buyer? _____

_____

_____

_____

_____

_____

3. Central buyers and category managers? _____

_____

_____

_____

_____

_____

4. Product managers and product sourcers? _____

_____

_____

_____

_____

(Continued)

Name _____

5. Executive trainee and training supervisor? _____

_____

_____

_____

_____

_____

6. Buyer's clerical and merchandise manager? _____

_____

_____

_____

_____

_____

7. Divisional merchandise manager (DMM) and general merchandise manager (GMM)? _____

_____

_____

_____

_____

_____

8. Fashion director and fashion consultant? _____

_____

_____

_____

_____

_____

9. Department manager and store manager? _____

_____

_____

_____

_____

_____

(Continued)

Name _____

10. Branch coordinators and distribution planners? _____

_____

_____

_____

_____

_____

11. District manager and regional manager of a chain store organization? _____

_____

_____

_____

_____

_____

12. Head of stock and customer service manager? _____

_____

_____

_____

_____

_____

13. Merchandise management track and operations management track? _____

_____

_____

_____

_____

_____

14. Loss prevention managers and information technology (IT) employees? _____

_____

_____

_____

_____

_____

Check It Out: Retail Job Availability

Activity B   **Name** _____

Chapter 28   **Date** _____ **Period**_____

Check out retail job availability in your town, county, and state or region. Look at want-ads in newspapers and online, contact employment agencies, and call the human resource offices of retail companies. Report on each of the following:

1. What are the different kinds of jobs available in the companies?

   _____

   _____

   _____

2. What education, training, and experience are required for the jobs?

   _____

   _____

   _____

3. Describe the pay for each job level.

   _____

   _____

   _____

4. Describe other parts of each compensation package, such as health insurance, merchandise discount, etc.

   _____

   _____

   _____

5. Describe a typical work schedule, such as weekends, holidays, etc.

   _____

   _____

   _____

6. How much competition exists for the various jobs?

   _____

   _____

   _____

7. Share other interesting facts you have discovered.

   _____

   _____

   _____

A Closer Look

Activity C

Name _____

Chapter 28

Date _____ **Period**_____

Analyze and compare four different retail careers described in this chapter by filling out the following. Then find other classmates who chose the same careers and compare your answers with theirs. As a group, discuss each career in class.

1. Employee's title: _____

   Preparation needed: _____

   _____

   _____

   Duties and responsibilities: _____

   _____

   _____

   Average salary or pay range: _____

   Typical work hours: _____

   Advantages: _____

   _____

   _____

   Disadvantages: _____

   _____

   _____

2. Employee's title: _____

   Preparation needed: _____

   _____

   _____

   Duties and responsibilities: _____

   _____

   _____

   Average salary or pay range: _____

   Typical work hours: _____

   Advantages: _____

   _____

   _____

(Continued)

Name _____

Disadvantages: _____

_____

_____

3. Employee's title: _____

   Preparation needed: _____

   _____

   _____

   Duties and responsibilities: _____

   _____

   _____

   Average salary or pay range: _____

   Typical work hours: _____

   Advantages: _____

   _____

   _____

   Disadvantages: _____

   _____

   _____

4. Employee's title: _____

   Preparation needed: _____

   _____

   _____

   Duties and responsibilities: _____

   _____

   _____

   Average salary or pay range: _____

   Typical work hours: _____

   Advantages: _____

   _____

   _____

   Disadvantages: _____

   _____

   _____

Check It Out: Fashion Curriculums

Activity D

Name _____

Chapter 28

Date _____ **Period** _____

Check out trade schools, junior colleges, and universities locally and in other parts of the country that offer fashion merchandising and/or retailing curriculums. Obtain information from different schools. Start by looking in the guides to trade schools and colleges in your school's counseling office or library. Most schools also have websites. Request catalogs from the schools. Then report on each of the following.

1. What are the admission requirements?

   _____

   _____

   _____

   _____

2. How would you apply?

   _____

   _____

   _____

3. What are the costs?

   _____

   _____

4. Is financial aid available?

   _____

5. Describe the size and location of each school.

   _____

   _____

6. What are the specifics (courses, time to completion, etc.) about their fashion-related curriculums?

   _____

   _____

   _____

   _____

   _____

7. What degrees are earned in the programs?

   _____

   _____

   _____

(Continued)

Name_____

8. What jobs/careers could graduates pursue?

_____

_____

_____

9. Describe student life and extracurricular opportunities.

_____

_____

_____

_____

10. Share other interesting facts you have discovered.

_____

_____

_____

_____

_____

_____

_____

_____

_____

_____

_____

_____

_____

_____

_____

_____

_____

_____

Retail Career Presentations

Activity E   Name _____

Chapter 28   Date _____ Period_____

Working in small groups, choose one of the following activities. Review the chapter section that is concerned with the activity and do additional research as needed. Present your information to the class. Group members should tape signs to themselves to show what function or job they represent.

- A. Review the three main functions of fashion merchandising for the rest of the class. Describe the many retail jobs that are involved in each of them.

- B. Describe both a two-functional and three-functional organization. Outline the duties and significance of each job.

- C. Represent the five main functional managers of a large retail organization. Describe the responsibilities for each of the managers and what falls within their jurisdictions.

- D. Describe the merchandise management career track from Executive Trainee to Vice President of Merchandising. Stand in order of responsibility and pay, from bottom to top, and describe the duties of each job.

- E. Describe the operations management career track from Executive Trainee to Vice President of Operations. Stand in order of responsibility and pay, from bottom to top, and describe the duties of each job.

- F. Describe to the class a small, traditional department store structure that has three specific departments. Describe the duties and significance of jobs in each department.

The letter of my group is: _____

Assignments for my group include:

Student #	Title of Role of Responsibility	Name of Student
1.		
2.		
3.		
4.		
5.		
6.		
7.		
8.		

Promotion

Careers

Promotion Review

Activity A   Name _____

Chapter 29   Date _____   Period_____

Answer the following questions as you review the chapter.

1. Where is mannequin work done by models? _____

    _____

    _____

2. Why is there a growing demand for older models, average to larger models, or models with disabilities?

    _____

    _____

3. What should models do to maintain their health and fitness? _____

    _____

    _____

4. What two types of organizations train models? _____

    _____

    _____

5. What types of poses are recommended for photos when registering with a modeling agency?

    _____

    _____

6. For what types of organizations do fashion journalists work? _____

    _____

    _____

7. What educational requirements are needed to become a fashion writer? _____

    _____

    _____

(Continued)

Name_____

8. Where are most fashion journalism jobs located? _____
   _____
   _____

9. What do textile firm fashion illustrators show in their drawings? _____
   _____
   _____

10. What higher education courses are especially needed for audiovisual work? _____
    _____
    _____

11. What is visual merchandising intended to show to customers? _____
    _____
    _____

12. Name three types of themes that a display designer might emphasize. _____
    _____
    _____
    _____

13. What can retailers do for displays if they do not have their own visual merchandising department?
    _____
    _____

14. Besides preparing retail print and broadcast advertisements, name three other advertising materials
    that might be prepared. _____
    _____
    _____

15. What types of bargaining and deals do media buyers transact with media salespeople? _____
    _____
    _____

16. Why are the jobs of layout artist and pasteup/mechanical artist disappearing? _____
    _____
    _____

17. Who does the public relations for large retail companies, chain organizations, and small stores?
    _____
    _____
    _____

Promotion Career Fill-In

Activity B   Name _____

Chapter 29   Date _____ Period _____

Fill in the open squares of the chart to write the terms described in the numbered definitions.

1.							F											
2.							A											
3.							S											
4.							H											
5.							I											
6.							O											
7.							N											

8.							P											
9.							R											
10.							O											
11.							M											
12.							O											
13.							T											
14.							I											
15.							O											
16.							N											

17.							C											
18.							A											
19.							R											
20.							E											
21.							E											
22.							R											
23.							S											

1. _____ models are design room or showroom models who try on and model samples for company management and retail buyers.

2. _____ models pose in front of cameras for pictures used in press releases or advertisements of manufacturers and other firms.

3. Photo _____ book models, accessorize apparel, obtain props, pin up hems, iron garments, and pick up and return merchandise for fashion photo shoots.

4. _____ designers are advertising employees who come up with the visual representations for advertisements and collateral materials.

(Continued)

Name _____

5. _____ are public relations agents who help companies project their public images.

6. Fashion _____ are fashion writers for the media.

7. Display _____ head retail display staffs and oversee all display work.

8. _____ compose the word messages that describe items that are being promoted in advertisements, catalogs, and brochures.

9. _____ directors are retail employees who supervise advertising departments and publications.

10. _____ artists are advertising employees who design the layouts for ads.

11. _____ buyers are advertising employees who select and buy the best media for clients' ads.

12. Fashion _____ are writers who pass along fashion information through the mass media.

13. Art _____ are advertising designers who conceptualize ads for newspapers, magazines, direct-mail flyers, radio, television, signs, outdoor media, and websites.

14. _____ work is employment doing radio, television, and multimedia presentations.

15. _____ executives are advertising agency employees in charge of selling to and handling specific advertising accounts.

16. _____ models work in fashion shows in front of live audiences.

17. _____ materials include extra advertising or corporate image pieces, such as brochures, annual reports, packaging, hangtags, logos, and trademarks.

18. Paste-up/_____ artists are advertising agency employees who put together the actual elements of ad layouts.

19. _____ supervise fashion writers and copywriters of publications.

20. Display _____ plan and put together retail displays.

21. Public _____ agents tell firms' stories to stockholders and the press.

22. Fashion _____ are artists who draw garments that have been designed and produced by others.

23. Window _____, also called window trimmers, plan and put together window displays.

Career Groupings

Activity C   **Name** _____

Chapter 29   **Date** _____ **Period**_____

A. Circle the general promotion category from the following that most interests you as a career.

    Modeling   Fashion writing   Fashion advertising

    Fashion photography   Visual merchandising   Public relations

B. Form small groups with the others from the class who have chosen the same career category. Discuss that career option and respond to the following statements.

   1. The specific jobs within that career category are: _____

      _____

      _____

      _____

   2. The types of duties and responsibilities in the career category include: _____

      _____

      _____

      _____

   3. The education and training requirements include: _____

      _____

      _____

      _____

   4. Advancement opportunities might be: _____

      _____

      _____

      _____

   5. The compensation to be expected at various levels is: _____

      _____

      _____

      _____

   6. The types of locations where these jobs exist include: _____

      _____

      _____

      _____

(Continued)

Name_____

7. The working conditions would probably be: _____

_____

_____

_____

8. Job security would probably be: _____

_____

_____

_____

9. The status/prestige in this career category is: _____

_____

_____

_____

C. After finishing the group discussion, fill out the following from strictly your own point of view.

10. The main advantages for you in this career are: _____

_____

_____

_____

11. The possible disadvantages for you in this career are: _____

_____

_____

_____

12. What comments do you have about making this your lifetime employment? _____

_____

_____

_____

A Fashion Interview

Activity D   **Name** _____

Chapter 29   **Date** _____ **Period** _____

For a mock television talk show, write out five questions you would ask a fashion expert (well-known designer, retail executive, magazine editor, etc.) in an interview. Then research this year's fashion trends, colors, fabrics, textures, accessories, and industry information needed to answer the questions. Get together with a classmate to combine your questions and add more depth of substance. Finally, with one of you asking the questions and the other assuming the identity of the fashion expert, hold an exclusive interview in front of the class. Have other students with interests in promotion record the interview with audio or video equipment as if you were conducting an actual radio or television broadcast.

1. _____
_____
_____
_____
_____

2. _____
_____
_____
_____
_____

3. _____
_____
_____
_____
_____

4. _____
_____
_____
_____
_____

5. _____
_____
_____
_____
_____

Entrepreneurship and Other Fashion-Related Careers

You as an Entrepreneur

Activity A Name _____

Chapter 30 Date _____ Period_____

Studies have shown that successful entrepreneurs possess high degrees of two specific traits:

- Lots of **nerve** enables people to control their environment rather than be controlled by it.

- A strong **urge for achievement** motivates them to show their effectiveness and gain success.

To calculate your aptitude, respond to the statements below. You will not be graded on your responses. Place checks in the appropriate columns. Give yourself 4 points if you strongly agree with the statement, 3 points if you generally agree, 2 points if you disagree somewhat, and 1 point if you strongly disagree.

NERVE:	**I strongly agree** (4 pts.)	**I generally agree** (3 pts.)	**I generally disagree** (2 pts.)	**I strongly disagree** (1 pt.)
I can do almost anything I set my mind to do.				
What happens to me in the future depends on me.				
I feel that my effort can successfully influence the outcome of a project.				
I can bring a change to many of the important things in my life.				
I rarely feel helpless in dealing with the problems of life.				
I don't let myself be pushed around.				
Subtotals				

(Continued)

Name _____

URGE FOR ACHIEVEMENT:	I strongly agree (4 pts.)	I generally agree (3 pts.)	I generally disagree (2 pts.)	I strongly disagree (1 pt.)
I always work hard to be the best at any work or activity.				
It is hard for me to forget about my work when I'm away from it.				
I find it hard to totally relax when on vacation.				
I would rather work with a difficult, highly-competent partner than with a congenial, less-competent one.				
I feel angry when I see waste or inefficiency on the job.				
I am annoyed when people are late for appointments.				
Subtotals				

Total your overall score to determine your entrepreneurial aptitude. If your total score is between 36 and 48, you have a high aptitude for becoming a successful entrepreneur. If your total score is between 24 and 35, you could probably be successful with your own business, but it might be difficult for you. If your total score is under 24, you would probably be more comfortable as an employee than as the owner of a business.

My total score is _____, which means

_____

Does this correspond with your previous thoughts about being an entrepreneur? Why or why not?

_____

_____

_____

_____

_____

_____

_____

Job Qualifications

Activity B   Name _____

Chapter 30   Date _____   Period_____

Match each of the following job titles with the person whose qualifications best meet it.

_____ 1. Pedro graduated from college with a degree in history. He did not want to become a history teacher because he is somewhat shy and likes to work independently. He has always been interested in antiques. He went back to a university for a master's degree in textile science.

_____ 2. Serena has been employed in general internal sales and promotion jobs with a commercial pattern company for many years. She has a wonderful fashion sense and would now like to branch out to work with the retail fabric stores that sell the company's patterns.

_____ 3. Shawna worked up from showroom salesperson to showroom manager for a women's sportswear manufacturer when her children were younger. Now she would like to have a home office so she can go out on calls while the children are in school, be with them after school, and do her paperwork in the evenings. She is considering selling women's hosiery for different small producers of socks, pantyhose, and exercise tights.

_____ 4. Joshua has a high school diploma, but no higher education or training. His main family duty during the past few years has been to do the family laundry. In his spare time he likes to tie-dye his own T-shirts. Joshua is willing to do accurate work, is always polite, and takes direction well to operate machinery.

_____ 5. Sophia earned a bachelor's degree in Family and Consumer Sciences Education at the state university. She took many textiles and clothing courses because she enjoys fabrics and sewing. She is organized, likes to work with teenagers, and would like to spread her enthusiasm for fashion to others.

_____ 6. Joel experimented with sewing pants, shirts, and jackets different ways when he was younger, having learned basic sewing skills from his mom who is a seamstress. However, now he enjoys working at a computer rather than a sewing machine, and studied journalism in college. He has just been employed by a commercial pattern company.

A. apparel producer
B. classroom teacher
C. clothing specialist
D. conservator
E. dry cleaner
F. educational representative
G. fit model
H. independent sales representative
I. retail coordinator
J. technical writer

(Continued)

Name_____

_____ 7. Isabella has always been a creative person and has lots of fashion ideas that she sews into garments. She has been doing merchandising and marketing work for a large manufacturer, but likes to make her own decisions and feels she would be happiest if she were self-employed. Her friend is a supervisor at a nearby contract sewing factory and has arranged an appointment for Isabella to talk to the factory manager.

_____ 8. Ricardo has a bachelor's degree in business, but has discovered that he really likes to teach. He can't afford to go back to college for a teaching degree, but is very smart and has the ability to learn about products quickly. He is pursuing a job in which he could use both his knowledge of business promotion and his interest in teaching.

_____ 9. Ava lives in New York City. She has a well-proportioned figure in a standard size, but does not know how to sew or make patterns. She wants steady work with regular hours, and is about to start her new job at a commercial pattern company.

_____ 10. Ryan is an extension agent on a state university textiles and clothing staff. He enjoys traveling throughout the state, helping people with their clothing needs. At other times, he writes educational articles, appears on local radio and TV shows, and communicates clothing information throughout communities in other ways.

Which job in the above descriptions appeals the most to you and why? _____

_____

_____

_____

_____

_____

_____

_____

_____

_____

_____

_____

_____

_____

A Retail Start-Up

Activity C   Name _____

Chapter 30   Date _____   Period_____

With the entire class, plan the start-up of a small retail store. First, decide on its image and target customers, making sure your business idea satisfies a growing need in the market. Outline a preliminary business plan. Come up with a name for your store and a company logo. Analyze the strengths and weaknesses of any competitors so you can effectively compete with them. Determine your time line from now until the opening of the store. Provide good reasons why you are making all of your sound business decisions.

After making the original decisions as a class, divide into groups that will oversee the planning for the facility, finances, personnel, merchandise, and promotion. With all groups coordinating their ideas, prepare a more specific business plan. Each group should review the text chapters that relate to its category of work and conduct extra research as needed. Groups will also have to interact with each other to coordinate details throughout the entire project.

A. Facility Group: Check out the availability and cost (per square foot) of physical space to be rented or purchased. Decide what locale would be the best area, even if you don't know the exact location. Then use the space configuration of existing stores in that area or decide on your own dimensions of the space for your store. Plan the store's floor plan. In general, what types of renovations do you think would have to be done to suit most locations to your particular type of store? What furnishings and merchandise fixtures would be needed? Place them onto your floor plan. What colors and materials (walls, flooring, lighting, etc.) will be used? What other details must be determined?

B. Finance Group: How might the new venture obtain financing? Has the facility group considered the costs for space and renovations (rather than just the location and size)? Will there be enough money to hire the needed personnel, buy the original inventory, and promote the store? (Make sure none of the groups overspend!) What do you anticipate the monthly overhead costs for electricity, phone, etc., will be? Will there be some extra funds available in case of emergencies? What if sales don't meet the anticipated volume for needed income? What changes might have to be made in the future to keep the store open? Should the store accept credit cards? What other details are pertinent?

C. Personnel Group: What specific employees will be needed? What are the salaries or wages per hour for these employees? How will you find the employees and decide which ones to hire? (Develop a sample classified ad or help wanted poster.) How will the work scheduling be done to hold down costs, but to adequately fill personnel needs for heavy shopping times, evenings, weekends, holidays? (Prepare a sample schedule.) How will personnel be trained? What types of fringe benefits will the store offer? Develop policies about employee vacations, merchandise discount, dress code, etc. Are there any details you have forgotten?

D. Merchandise Group: Prepare a merchandise buying plan. When, where, and from whom will the merchandise buying be done? Will your store develop any private label goods? What retail pricing strategies will be used to try to maximize profits while perpetuating the store's image? How will merchandise be received by the store and placed onto the selling floor? Will there be guidelines about merchandise presentation (garment or color coordination, stock rotation, wall arrangements, ways to fold or hang items, etc.)? Have the right types and placement of fixtures been planned? What precautions will be taken against merchandise spoilage, shoplifting, and employee theft? Are there any other merchandising decisions to be made?

(Continued)

Name_____

E. Promotion Group: How will you promote the opening of your new store? What type of ongoing advertising will be done for the store and its products? How much will the advertising cost? Has the facility group allowed enough space for displays? Who will do your special displays? What props and equipment will be needed, and how much will it cost? Will you hold any special events? Describe them. What effective, unusual public relations techniques could you use to draw positive attention to the store? Should the store have a website? If so, what should be featured on it? Have you thought of everything?

After figuring out all the details and coordinating all the groups to plan your new store, **professionally present the finished plan** to your teacher, school administrators, parents, and/or guests. Dress in businesslike attire and use effective visual aids.

What are the most important concepts that you learned from this exercise? _____

_____

_____

_____

_____

_____

_____

_____

_____

_____

_____

_____

_____

_____

_____

_____

_____

_____

_____

_____

Read About Real Life

Activity D   **Name** _____

Chapter 30   **Date** _____   **Period** _____

Find an article in a newspaper, magazine, or online about someone in a career related to the content of this chapter. Attach the article to this page and respond to the following:

1. What are the skills needed to do the tasks of the job? _____

   _____

   _____

2. What education and training do you think the person has? _____

   _____

   _____

3. What background experience do you think the person has? _____

   _____

   _____

4. What would the person's working conditions and hours be? _____

   _____

   _____

5. What might the person's future career be like? _____

   _____

   _____

   _____

6. List what you think the advantages or rewards of the job are. _____

   _____

   _____

   _____

7. List what you think the disadvantages are. _____

   _____

   _____

   _____

8. Would this be a good job for you? Why or why not? _____

   _____

   _____

   _____

Match the Terms

Activity E   Name _____

Chapter 30   Date _____ Period_____

Match the following chapter terms and definitions by placing the correct letter next to each number.

_____ 1. A combination of teaching and business promotion.

_____ 2. An educator hired and paid by state land grant universities to work as a home economist in various counties or an entire state.

_____ 3. A person who gives instruction in school clothing and merchandising classes, extension work, and/or adult and consumer education courses.

_____ 4. Instructional courses held for adults at night.

_____ 5. The giving of special attention to taking long-term care of fabrics and clothing.

_____ 6. A theatrical wardrobe helper who organizes the costumes and accessories by character and scene.

_____ 7. The selling of a person's expert ideas and advice as a service business.

_____ 8. Commercial pattern company employee who does technical drawings to accompany the written directions of the guide sheet.

_____ 9. A person who organizes, launches, and directs a new business venture, and assumes the financial risks and uncertainties of the enterprise.

_____ 10. A person who locates, identifies, and determines the age of textiles, apparel, and accessories from the past.

_____ 11. An expert sewer who makes custom garments or does apparel alterations and repairs.

_____ 12. Wardrobing for operas, ballets, stage plays, circuses, movies, advertisements, television shows, and parades.

_____ 13. A written definition of the idea (purpose), operations, and financial forecast of an entrepreneur's proposed company.

_____ 14. Manufacturing that uses the labor of family units working in their homes with their own equipment.

_____ 15. The expenses to turn a new business venture into reality.

_____ 16. A sales employee of a home sewing material store.

_____ 17. A government agency that offers helpful counseling, workshops, videotapes, and free publications to entrepreneurs.

_____ 18. The selling of expert skills to accomplish particular tasks.

_____ 19. A firm that designs, produces, packages, and sells the patterns that are purchased by home sewers.

_____ 20. Head of a theatrical costume department.

A. adult education
B. business plan
C. commercial pattern company
D. consulting
E. consumer education
F. costume curator
G. costume technician
H. cottage industry
I. dressmaker/tailor
J. entrepreneur
K. extension agent
L. fabric store salesperson
M. fashion educator
N. freelancing
O. start-up costs
P. textile/apparel preservation
Q. theatrical costuming
R. U.S. Small Business Administration
S. wardrobe designer
T. diagram artist